SUN MYUNG MOON

and the Unification Church

SUN MYUNG MOON

and the Unification Church

FREDERICK SONTAG

Abingdon • Nashville

Sun Myung Moon and the Unification Church

Copyright © 1977 by Abingdon

Library of Congress Cataloging in Publication Data

SONTAG, FREDERICK.
  Sun Myung Moon and the Unification Church.
  Bibliography: p.
  1. Segye Kidokkyo T'ongil Sillyŏng Hyŏphoe.
2. Moon, Sun Myung. I. Title.
BX9750.S4S66   289.9   [B]   77-9075
                    ISBN 0-687-40622-6

Scripture quotation on the dedication page is from the
Jerusalem Bible, copyright © 1966 by Darton, Longman
& Todd, Ltd. and Doubleday & Company, Inc. Used by
permission of the publisher.

The Declaration of Theological Affirmations on pages
102-5 is quoted with the permission of the Unification
Theological Seminary at Barrytown, N.Y.

Selections from *Master Speaks* in chapter 5 are used with
permission of the Unification Church.

Lines from "The Impossible Dream" on page 213 are
from the musical play *Man of LaMancha* copyright ©
1965 by Andrew Scott, Inc., Helena Music Corporation,
and Sam Fox Publishing Company. Sam Fox Publishing
Company sole agent. Used by permission.

Photographs not otherwise noted courtesy the Unification Church.

Photographs noted UC/NFP courtesy Unification
Church/New Future Photographs.

MANUFACTURED BY THE PARTHENON PRESS AT
NASHVILLE, TENNESSEE, UNITED STATES OF AMERICA

Publisher's Preface

Since its beginning in Korea in 1946, the Unification Church, founded by Sun Myung Moon, has become one of the most controversial movements in this generation.

Any movement that arouses such widespread public attention and deep emotion needs exploration and study, not only as a journalistic sensation but as a phenomenon to be understood in its motivations as well as its manifestations.

Intrigued by questions about the origins of the movement and its continuing appeal to some young people of both East and West, the author, Frederick Sontag, has made a unique personal odyssey that has brought him into contact with hundreds of Moon followers and with Moon himself in a lengthy exclusive interview. The purpose of this book is not to examine in depth the serious criticism of the movement or to critically analyze or compare its doctrines with the major Christian theological viewpoints.

The views of the author are not necessarily those of the publisher; nor does publication imply endorsement or support of the Unification Church, its leaders, tenets, or activities.

For

GLF and NWF

and

their families

Catch the foxes for us,
the little foxes
that make havoc of the vineyards,
for our vineyards are in flower.
—Song of Songs 2:15
(Jerusalem Bible)

Other Books by Frederick Sontag

Divine Perfection: Possible Ideas of God

The Existentialist Prolegomena: To a Future Metaphysics

The Future of Theology: A Philosophical Basis for Contemporary Protestant Thought

The Problems of Metaphysics

The Crisis of Faith: A Protestant Witness in Rome

God, Why Did You Do That?

The God of Evil: An Argument from the Existence of the Devil

How Philosophy Shapes Theology: Problems in the Philosophy of Religion

The American Religious Experience: The Roots, Trends, and the Future of American Theology (with John Roth)

Love Beyond Pain: Mysticism Within Christianity

God and America's Future (with John Roth)

Contents

Introduction

Any reader who comes to this book looking for definite answers will be disappointed. In the first place, philosophers seldom give out such solutions. As fledgling philosophy students quickly learn to their dismay, we are much better at asking questions than at answering them. In the second place, the Moon phenomenon does not admit of easy solutions, and in some cases perhaps no solutions whatever are possible. Some quick questions asked by many about this controversial new religion can be answered easily by one who has studied the movement. As I reviewed the small mountain of transcriptions of the taped interviews I had accumulated, I noticed that the questions I asked frequently at first, I gradually ceased to ask as greater exposure made the answers clear to me.

However, more important and difficult questions emerged in trade for every simple issue I resolved. It is the theme of this book that those issues remaining are of such importance that all interested in religious life and the health of society would be wise to ponder them. Philosophers have long argued—and not been much thanked for doing so—that most people ask the wrong questions at first. I am convinced this is true where the Unification Church is concerned. Thus, it would be no small service if this book could put the hard questions on the right plane and in their most illuminating form.

Why should we pay serious attention to the Unification Church? There are many who do not think we should and others who think it is a passing phenomenon. The last chapter will try to balance the evidence on both sides of the

"At the alarming rate of spiritual decline in the West, it is conceivable that God is getting Koreans ready to serve as missionaries to the Western Church." Billy Graham, as quoted by Kurt Koch in *Victory Through Persecution*.

major issues, which is the best I think can be done. But in the course of my odyssey I did come to two firm conclusions: (1) The origins of the movement are genuinely humble, religious, and spiritual (which many doubt); and (2) the adaptability and solidarity of the movement are such that we are dealing with a movement here to stay. We have witnessed in our own lifetime the birth, growing pains— and will see the maturity—of a new religious movement.

What the movement has accomplished in a short time (thirty years) is rather phenomenal. From persecution and prison and a few converts, it began to grow in Seoul and moved to Japan, America, Europe, and on to 120 mission countries. In the mission countries, the numbers are very small, but nevertheless the church is there. From poverty it has grown to a business success that must make it one of the best-funded new religious movements. Its numbers are small, certainly no more than 500,000 core members in all countries. But each member works full time and often fulfills several functions at once. Associate members have been estimated at around two million. Whether positive or negative, it has attracted worldwide attention. It is a growth and success story to make Horatio Alger jealous and John D. Rockefeller glow with pride.

As I traveled, people outside of and hostile to the church took it for granted that I was out to write an exposé to destroy the movement; that is, if they thought I had a free mind. Members inside were sure I had come to save them from a hostile press and would eventually join as I too saw "the truth." As for myself, all I could see was an odyssey on which I had been launched, questions that grew and seemed to defy solutions, plus feeling a sense of wonder and a shudder of awe over what I had become involved in. Any movement capable of arousing such depth of emotion deserves your attention, as it held mine, long enough to penetrate the surface phenomena (for example, street fund raising), which are easily enough dismissed. Can anything good come out of Korea? we ask, just as an earlier age asked about Nazareth. The prejudice against South Korea is so strong that many answer no, without taking time to think.

Something has been stirring in the East in the form of Christian religious ferment, and we had better take a look at it. Kurt Koch informs us that "the four great revivals of recent decades have been gifts to non-European countries occurring in Korea (1906), Uganda (1927), Formosa (1945), and Indonesia (1965)."* Billy Graham undoubtedly did not

---

*Kurt Koch, *Victory Through Persecution* (Grand Rapids, Michigan: Kegel Publications, 1972), p. 25.

have Sun Myung Moon in mind at the time, but he is quoted by Koch as saying, "At the alarming rate of spiritual decline in the West, it is conceivable that God is getting Koreans ready to serve as missionaries to the Western Church" (preface). If Billy Graham also says, "The Korean Church stands as a beacon of Spiritual light in an era of darkness" (p. 25), it would pay us to take a close look at the Moon phenomenon for what it may teach us.

The materials on this project accumulated as if they were a rolling snowball. Mark Weatherly took over and organized these, cataloging the great variety into categories. Without this work of his, it would have been impossible to make effective use of all the materials that poured in. Kimberly Mueller typed most of the rough draft, and Betty Pierce coordinated the various aspects of the project. Pauline Bastien undertook the monumental task of transcribing more than forty, ninety-minute tapes of conversations and interviews, conducted in many languages and in as many foreign countries, often under less than ideal recording conditions. These reports in the words of the people who are themselves involved may form the greatest insight this book has to offer.

When I first heard of Sun Myung Moon, or any of the new religious cults, I had the tendency to lump them all together. I suspect most readers of news stories do this unconsciously. I eventually concentrated on Sun Moon partly because that is what the publishers asked me to do and partly because I knew that trying to understand one new cult would be difficult enough. However, having obtained a certain degree of comprehension of one, I am now convinced that one major difficulty in discussing any new religious movement is that the stories and doctrines of one get transferred to them all. For instance, reading Ted Patrick's book *Let Our Children Go* and hearing the account of his own experience with the Children of God sect, I realized that many of the things said about the Unification Church appear to be practices of the Children of God sect, judging by Patrick's account. The confusing thing is that many of the new movements do overlap, both in practice

14

and in doctrine. Thus, it takes more patience than most people are willing to practice to keep from blending one story into another. However, the reader will never understand the Moon movement unless he can do that, since it seems to be significantly different from most of the recent pop cults. The reader will have to practice concentration to block out other stories he has heard if he is to realize this.

It would not be possible to thank all who assisted in this project. Everyone in and out of my own family has become aware of the "Moon project" and taken some interest in it, pro or con—as befits such a controversial subject. Thousands of articles, comments, and questions poured in, including at least a hundred title suggestions involving some play on the name *Moon*. The movement has something at some point to intrigue or infuriate everyone. The project has of necessity been a "lived through" event. It could not have been done otherwise. The book grew into a "tiger on my back."

Particularly, however, I must avoid thanking any one individual in the Unification Church, official or member. As the book explains, their cooperation in providing access was crucial. Hospitality has been offered me in church centers around the world. I seldom asked for a piece of material that I did not receive. If there was resistance to any of my inquiries, I did not detect it. The movement has a tradition, perhaps derived from the East, of providing hospitality to a guest, and I found myself always treated in this way. Lacking such auspices, the background research for this book would have been impossible. But any report on my findings requires that the book begin by explaining itself.

I invite the reader to make a journey with me through the labyrinth.

I thought of a labyrinth of labyrinths, of one sinuous spreading labyrinth that would encompass the past and the future and in some way involve the stars.

—Jorge Luis Borges

How and Why
This Book Was Written

A Cultural, Spiritual, and Political Adventure

Like many others, I first heard about the Reverend Sun Myung Moon through newspaper stories of a somewhat sensational character. These centered on the objections of parents whose children, they said, had been "stolen." Next, like some other scholars and professors, I found myself one day with material on my desk inviting me to attend the Fourth International Conference on the Unity of the Sciences (ICUS) in New York City in November of 1975. I recognized that the conference was sponsored by the Cultural Foundation of the Unification Church and that the Reverend Sun Moon was the founder.

Unlike some, I was not put off by this. On the contrary, I was intrigued to find out more. As it turned out, from the date of my somewhat innocent acceptance until the time of the conference itself, the first major furor in the newspapers and magazines of America took place. During most of this period I was away from California. But one day I received a telephone call in Hawaii from conference headquarters in New York, asking if I would become the chairman of the committee to which I had submitted a paper. I questioned the last-minute invitation and was given a rather lengthy explanation—by long-distance telephone—about various negative pressures in the press concerning the conference and the subsequent withdrawal of some of its leaders, including the chairman of my committee. Since the conversation was open and the explanation seemed frank and was accompanied by an offer to send me all of the relevant articles that had appeared in the press, I could see no reason to withdraw at that point. I felt myself interested in finding out what might be at the bottom of all the controversy.

Becoming chairman of my small committee was a fairly innocuous project, but attending the conference brought the participants into contact with newspaper reporters and the protest pickets outside the hotel. As the mystery deepened, I began to acquire literature on the church and the movement. Like the comment of one newspaper reporter, I found myself learning more and more but getting further away from any final answer. "Learned ignorance," Nicholas Cusanus called it in mystical talk. By then I had seen enough members of the movement to know that the hostile attitude of press articles could not be founded in 100 percent truth, or the church would not be as successful as it obviously was.

As I came into contact with the younger members of the church, most of them in their early twenties, I found myself struck by a rather attractive quality in their candid eagerness to talk about their church. One thinks of Moon's church as a somewhat secretive organization, but on contact this did not seem to be the case. I heard that the church had formed a seminary, and I mentioned that I would like to visit and speak to the student body. This invitation subsequently came, and I spent one day at Barrytown, New York, lecturing and talking informally with the students.[1] I found them open, loquacious, and, on the whole, well-informed. As a result, I wrote a short article about the church,[2] since it seemed to raise questions that the accounts in the public press had not come near explaining.

Because these unsolved puzzles intrigued me, and because I felt the Science Conference could be more effectively organized, given the time and money they

---

[1] My companion on the return trip to New York City was an ardent spokesman for the church who is now a prominent deprogrammer at the Tucson center. We have communicated since, and he is as rigidly con Moon now as he was pro then.

[2] See "The New Moon Sophistry" in *Religion in Life*, Autumn 1977.

expended on it, I accepted a major role in their next affair, to be held in Washington, D.C., in 1976. In the course of meeting to plan for this conference, we were informed that Reverend Moon (as he has come to be known) had invited the group to dinner at his home. This was an unusual evening. I reported the whole experience to a friend, who quietly filed a note to himself to mention it to the editors of Abingdon Press, since they have an interest in reporting on new religious movements.

At their request, I put the draft of my article into the hands of the Abingdon editors. Subsequently they asked me if I would consider doing a book on the church which expanded on the theme of the article. This meant developing neither an exposé nor a defense of the church but rather examining the questions that the success of the movement raises for all of us involved in theology and religion. For instance, when a plethora of new religious movements of somewhat strange origins spring up and flourish, does this signal the failure of our culture and its established religious institutions as it often has in the past?

When the contract was offered, I replied that I would be interested in doing a book only if the Unification Church itself would cooperate by making its centers open to me. I wanted to interview members and visit their centers to see the life of the church from inside. Eventually church headquarters responded and said that, yes indeed, they would be happy to cooperate on such a project. We agreed that I would spend a week at their headquarters on the East Coast and visit the source of the church in Korea and Japan. Since I was on my way to Europe for the summer at the American Church in Paris anyway, I would start by visiting the major centers of the European church.

I insisted on staying in the church's centers, except in Korea and Japan, where they are not equipped for Western guests. In this way I had an opportunity to get a feeling for the actual life-style of the people living there. After returning home from the summer in Europe, my program with the church and my publishers was to: (1) explore some of the centers in America and attend a weekend training session as a participant; (2) revisit the Barrytown seminary for interviews; (3) interview as many church leaders in America as possible; (4) attend the Washington Monument rally as a spectator; (5) visit Japan and Korea to search out the movement's origins and early growth; (6) contact as many ex-members and anti-Moon organizations as possible to gather their literature; and, then, (7) end with an extended interview with Reverend Moon. All this was done.

Who Is to Be Believed?

Once I had agreed to do this project, I began to save every press account and magazine story I could find. Friends who knew of my interest daily showered me with clippings. These run to 122 major stories, discounting duplication. I have no idea what the total would be if every item that appeared were included in the count, but surely it would fill a small room. As these came in I read them over, but I also wanted to review the mass collectively to try to put the pieces together. I took this large file along as my project when my wife and I left Paris and traveled to Copenhagen by train.

I expected great revelations as I began to go through the accumulated stack. Instead, the train had not left French territory before I realized that, give or take a few items, all the stories sounded alike, and the substance was really the same. Then, as I visited the centers and began to see a different side of the movement, I puzzled more and more over the uniformity and similarity of the press accounts. No doubt there are many explanations that could be given. *Newsweek* magazine had done extensive research for a comprehensive cover story, and, when I posed this puzzle about the uniformity of the press coverage, one of their editors explained the facts of newspaper and magazine life to me. Few writers and editors have time, he said, for much extensive, on-site investigation, so they borrow from one another's stories. Once an account is printed, it tends to be repeated and believed just because it is in print.

This phenomenon is not confined to "yellow journals" but applies to all media. When I pressed the editors of *Der Spiegel* about their source for one oft-repeated charge about Moon's early sex practices, they replied, as if it solved the mystery, "But we read that in the *New York Times*!" A book could be written about press attitudes and how truth gets communicated in newsprint, but that is a side, if nevertheless challenging, issue. All I want to do is call to the reader's attention the difficulty involved in achieving objectivity where anything so subject to bias as Sun Myung Moon is concerned.

A Journey Through the Labyrinth

Now I have traveled half the world, gathered a small mountain of material, taped interviews with literally dozens of people, seen most of the church centers and activities, and met almost all of its leaders, past and present. Many of the early, often-asked questions are easily answered, but in their place loom a hundred more difficult issues. The mystery deepens because anyone who goes through all this becomes aware that it is a complex involving nearly every tangled problem of our day. You are wandering through a labyrinth.

What is fascinating about the movement is that the problems of the day are mirrored in it, whether social, religious, political, or psychological. Evaluate the Unification Church movement adequately and you have understood our era. This church raises the issues of the deterioration of our family structure, the lethargy of many traditional religious institutions, the problem of religions intruding their goals into politics, and the religious control of money and power. At the center of it all lies the question of Jesus and his mission, plus the perplexing issue of how God acts and whether he gives new revelations in a new day.

The question of "truth" is involved, which is the philosopher's ancient quest. I found some truth in every negative charge made against the church and at the same time much truth in the church members' internal life and doctrine. No answer that dismisses or "exposes" them is sufficient, since it fails to explain why the movement flourishes and has spread so widely. No "deprogramming" campaign explains why many who are kidnapped voluntarily return, and no charge of "political front" explains the religious origins of the movement and its insistence on prayer and God at the center of the members' lives.

One can talk to bitter ex-members whose obsession now is to drag members out and to destroy the movement when only yesterday their avowed mission was to bring the kingdom of God on earth. One must ponder which obsession is better. One can see individuals who have been mentally shaken by their experience but also talk to dozens inside who proclaim the movement as the saving force in their life. One can hear stories involving deception in street selling and then experience the apparent openness of most members. Tie all this together with their anti-Communist commitment and the church's desire to mobilize the political sector to join their drive to inaugurate God's kingdom on earth and you have a puzzle.

The difficult phenomenon that any simple notion of truth must account for is that one can take almost every statement made and read it positively or negatively, depending on one's basic values. For instance, "they are kept too busy to see their families" can be positive, *if* you believe the youth are working tirelessly to bring the kingdom of heaven on earth. "They are changed so that I can't recognize my own son" can be translated "They have become converted and experienced spiritual rebirth," *if* you accept spiritual transformation as the aim of all religion. Or, "Moon demands slavish obedience" can become "They have learned discipline and the need to consider others before themselves."

Is one forced to take one side or the other and become either ardently pro or ardently con? Beneath the whole array of charges and countercharges is truth buried so deep that we can never hope to view it directly? Are these problems forced on us only to transcend our grasp? As Kant said in the preface to the First Critique: "Human reason has this peculiar fate that in one species of its knowledge it is burdened by questions which, as prescribed by the very nature of reason itself, it is not able to ignore, but which, as transcending all its powers, it is also not able to answer."

"No one I know has anything good to say about Reverend Moon," reports my wife, and one has only to mention his name to see the negative reaction aroused. Face an aroused mob in the Yale Divinity School Commons Room, which includes both Moonies and hostile parents, as I did, and you get some sense of how deep the feelings run. To those opposed, anything but a vow to destroy the church is a sell-out, while inside the movement, members have trouble understanding why their actions arouse such antagonism.

During the question period of the talk I gave in the Yale Divinity School series on new religious movements, one ex-member shouted at me in anger, "You've either been duped or paid off!" I don't remember what point I had been making at the time, but for anyone in the opposition camp dedicated to destroying the movement, one's motives must be suspect if one is not out to "expose" corruption in the Unification Church. "I gather you're rather positive," a psychiatric social worker said to me at the end of a long phone conversation. I translated this to mean that I manage to see something positive in the mixture and had not yet vowed to destroy the movement.

After speaking to another group about Moon, a friend took me aside and said, "Fred, if you think you've encountered opposition in trying to do the investigation for this book, I want to warn you that when the book comes out, if it says anything positive about Reverend Moon, this will commit an unpardonable sin in the eyes of the 'liberal religious establishment,' and you will be written off." A member of my family asked me, "Do you feel as if you're on the church's payroll?" We must ask ourselves to what limits we will go in order to discredit a witness who goes against deeply set beliefs, whose upset threatens a whole way of life.

As for myself, I have accepted and appreciated the church's hospitality as their guest at centers all over the

23

world. When one of the movement's leading opponents questioned me on this, I asked her how else I was to see and experience the church from the inside. She seemed content with this answer, but I suspect others will not be. In discussing with a friend the dilemma of how one could see the movement from the inside without being accused of being bribed, he remarked that any anthropologist who wants to study a community works to gain its acceptance in order to live among them so as to experience their life from inside. However, living with a primitive tribe in New Zealand does not arouse the emotion and hostility that living with the Moonies does.

In negotiating to do this book, the church agreed on its part to open its doors and give me access to any person or any material. I can only report that no significant request has been turned down and that I feel I have had open access to speak to every early witness and present leader. I suppose this could all be an elaborate set-up on their part, using Descartes's evil demon to deceive me with a contrived set of actors. All I can say is that the stories I have heard ring true, although not without vast complications and questions. The issue is whether this gives me valid insight into the church or simply makes me into one deceived by them. You must judge for yourself.

In philosophy, of course, we call such charges *ad hominem* arguments, directed to the man and not to the issue. It is not my intent to direct any reader's attention to the author except that the issue of credibility has arisen and will arise. My hope is to focus your attention to the serious problems that the success of the movement brings to light, and then to direct all our energy toward meeting these needs rather than in wasted warfare bent on destroying our enemies, a scene we witness in Ireland and Lebanon with all too much pain.

One long-time, and quite sane, Unification Church member said to me in response to my question of what Reverend Moon meant to him: "He is a mirror in which I see myself—as I should and would like to be." However, in regard to the question of the credibility of this report, my aim is to ask the reader to consider Sun Myung Moon as a mirror in which every ill of modern man and contemporary society can be seen. Reverend Moon proposes one cure—his own. The real issue is not his credibility or the author's supposed acquired blindness but the discovery of the ills of our soul and of society as they are reflected here. Next, we must work to give a better answer and to propose our own cure for spiritual illness rather than waste our energy in destroying the annoying revealer.

What Do the People Say in Europe?

Come, ye people all around the world,
let's unite into one.

—from a Unification Church song

The reports of those who have had a bad experience with the movement speak to us in the multitude of sensational stories that flow from the press. To balance out the puzzle, we should listen to reports from Moon's followers before we try to evaluate the negative attacks. Of course, the comments reported in chapters 2, 3, and 4 come mostly from "the best side" of the church, although I interviewed ex-members and strongly antichurch forces, too. What is little understood by an outsider is the deeply spiritual side of the movement. Perhaps the words of the members themselves best exemplify this. The quotations used represent high points, but the standard exposé treats the movement as if it had no genuinely spiritual core. No religious group has only successful members. Some less than ideal experiences can be found to match each one that is good.

The quotations I have used are taken from taped interviews organized according to the country in which the interviews took place or, in some cases, the home base of the individual if I caught up with him or her in another country. I have listed only the city and country of the interview site, and I agreed to quote no one by name. The point of interest is not the individual person but his or her perspective on the church. In many cases, a group was

26

present, and it was not possible to identify each speaker by name. The responses have been left in their original order, since rearranging them according to theme seemed to destroy the impressionistic flavor. In some cases, the comment came in response to my questions, but often the most significant and illuminating ones appeared spontaneously in the course of the discussion. Thus, if I cited my specific question in each case, it would often be out of place.

In each case, I asked extensive questions about the financing of the church, the members fund-raising activities, their street witnessing, their mission work, and the various aims of the church in that country, as well as its current strength. With the possible exception of the sale of ginseng tea, which seems a consistent worldwide money raiser, there is no single pattern of fund raising. It is different in each country and for each stage of growth.

Quite often, fund raising involves selling a newspaper or pamphlet, the price of which in effect becomes a donation to the church. Sometimes members operate a printing business and sell the cards they make. In other cases, they are more extensively involved in actual manufacture and industry. Candles are a favorite home product. Sometimes a few members will keep outside jobs and contribute all or part of their salary to the upkeep of the church. It appears that the financial stability of the church varies exactly in proportion to the financial success or stability of the country. In other words, in Europe, Germany is perhaps the most successful and well-funded; France, second in line, England and Italy, a little lower on the ladder, but all still successful. A smaller country like Denmark has a marginal mission operation.

If I had not already been committed to spend the summer in Europe, I probably would never have visited the Unification Church headquarters in those countries. In retrospect, it appears a stroke of fortune that I was exposed to the church in a foreign setting before coming home to begin the American investigation. We arrived in France just after the fourth of July, where I would be interim pastor at the American Church in Paris. Using the American Church as our base, my wife and I traveled to England and later spent several days in Holland. Finally, I went to Germany and Italy and ended with a somewhat longer stay in Copenhagen.

Counting members, the Unification Church in Europe is not large, perhaps at most a few thousand. For instance, the editors of *Der Spiegel* told me they did not fear the church in Germany because it was too small. On hearing this, most people miss the fact that almost all those who join, join for full-time duty. The closest comparison is probably that of a co-ed monastic order. That is, male and female members live together in a family, but as brothers and sisters—a pattern perfected in Japan. Most give up their personal lives for the work of the church. Thus, a few members can be much more effective than the much larger congregation of an ordinary Protestant or Catholic church in which the members devote only a small amount of time to church activities. Each Unification member is, in effect, an ordained minister. But more important than that, he or she is a full-time missionary, spreading the work of the church, and most of them work at top speed and around the clock.

The structure of the church in Europe is similar in each country. In each major city, there are houses that serve as hospitality or reception centers. People who become interested in the church are invited to come and study further for a short period. Usually this means a weekend at a training center in a countryside setting. Those who become more serious and whose interest is sustained are next invited to attend for periods of a week or longer. As has been noted many times by the press, these city centers, and particularly the training centers, are often in physically beautiful situations. The buildings themselves are attractive, and they become more so as the movement succeeds.

This is not an unusual pattern. When one examines the situation among most Roman Catholic religious orders, one finds monasteries and nunneries often located in imposing and physically attractive settings. As a monk friend of mine once said when I visited his monastery on a bluff overlooking the Pacific, "We Roman Catholics have an eye for a nice piece of real estate." On the other hand, many of Moon's small city centers are quite simple and modest in appearance. In the early days, they all were, but success has changed that.

To illustrate my point of the mobility and international character of the movement, here is an interview that took place in New York, although the individual speaking was central to the expansion of the movement in several European countries. He is European but now operates mission teams in various countries, at present in the United States.

New York City. Interview with early European leader in the Unification Church. November 1976.

"When someone who didn't know the *Divine Principle* starts studying it, he discovers things he had never discovered before. For instance, he will discover very realistically that God exists. That is an enormous discovery—not a belief—it is a discovery. And through this discovery his whole relationship to the world changes. Things that were important before are suddenly not that important. And other things become very important. So his whole measurement instantly changes. Because of this change, this person reacts very differently also, to his relatives and everybody. But the other people cannot understand it. They think the person must be brainwashed. But the person just found something he never expected to find. . . .

"We want not to separate but to unify. Therefore, if people say that we are separating children from their parents, this would be the exact opposite of our goal. . . .

"The young people who are coming are very attracted because they find something they didn't find at home. You see, when you taste once fully the love of God, you must be drawn to God more than to all other things. . . .

"Our church has received the instruction from God to unify the world. So in the next ten years this will happen in the most unexpected, most unusual way. We will be unified. The church will play a major role. . . . The urgency of God's will is comparable to the ark of Noah. He had only a limited time to build it. The waters were coming. And I strongly believe we are living a similar time. But the people don't see that. They don't see the urgency. We see it. We see the trouble we are running into in the world. I know we have only a short time. But the people are not ready. . . .

"The mission [of the church] can never fail. For the success of this mission in this time, a few things had to be established, and those things have been established. In the fight between good and evil, the good side has already won enough so that the good side now can conquer the world."

France

Because I was scheduled to spend a month in Paris at the American Church, I had an opportunity to examine the church and its activities in France in greater depth than in other countries where I spent less time. We had lunch one day at the downtown Paris headquarters of the Unification Church, which included an extended conversation with the dozen or so members. The meal served was very French. The group was quiet and somewhat reticent, although they had already experienced sensational press stories and a bombing of their headquarters.

Paris. Luncheon with French church members. July 1976.

"The mission of the church is, I think, to bring on earth the ideal of God, the will of God, and to put it into practice, to change the world so that all people can live a happy life."

"Everything that is divided we want to unite. The first thing to do is to find unity with God, a personal relationship with God."

"Traditional Christianity has left many points in darkness; many things are not clear about God, about the origin of evil and the ideal of man. I think the *Divine Principle* reveals to us many points, many new points."

"I think people have never seen a church like ours. We are not retiring from society. We are in it, and that is why people sometimes think, oh, it is a political religious sect or movement."

"We give people outside the appearance of being rich, of being able to do anything, to have the money to do anything. They don't know the difference between power and spiritual force. The spirit is the most important to us. They don't understand that."

"When people tell us we are not Christians, I realize actually much more than before what Christ's mission was."

"Now I know the Messiah is a key, a mediator, a door, a gate. But in fact the ideal of God is each one should become a messiah, a true son of God. Now the question is if Reverend Moon, after Jesus, is the one among so many. Only you yourself can answer that. If I make a theory—Mr. Moon is such and such—that is of no value. Our mission is just to give testimony about what we experience."

"I think we all expect to see the world change in our lifetime. Of course, we always think the world will change very quickly, and we all expect that we can do it. Now exactly what will happen and how it will happen I have no idea. I think the important thing is to go as far as possible. I am sure God himself does not know exactly what will happen. If he knew, it would mean that man is not free. Everything depends on man's response."

"All during history we have been walking in a very long tunnel. Our job is very simple. It is just to show the people that we are the exit."

Next, I traveled further north to the major training center near Rouen. It is a chateau in the process of reconstruction, where small groups, somewhat international in character, as befits the Paris university scene, were engaged in a training session. During that day, there was a chance to talk to the older members of the church who operate the sessions, as well as to those who were new to the church and were there only for the weekend to learn something further. One interesting person participating in the discussion was a young man who had almost completed training to become a Jesuit priest before he joined the movement.

Rouen, France. Conversation at the training center. July 1976.

"I felt that with this kind of people I could do something. We are trained to be a new type of family, a new type of society."

"I think the experience of God is much more alive in the Unification Church."

31

"I thought, if God wants to make a complete change today, and if Christians don't respond, maybe God has to show the way by another movement, another group."

"I want to understand what God is doing. If I am wrong, I will recognize that later. But if it is the truth, it is such an important responsibility for me that I cannot escape it. I want to take my responsibility."

On another occasion, we traveled south to Lyon to spend two days. We were able to talk both to the local group and also to a mobile mission fund-raising team with headquarters in Lyon. This group included the girl who is now celebrated in the French church because of the TV and newspaper pictures taken when her mother first called the media and then publicly kidnapped her daughter away

PHOTO BY AUTHOR

PHOTO BY BRACEY HOLT

Left: French Moonies at Lyon sing a farewell song for the author.
Right: French publications.

from the church. The girl later returned and is still a member.

Lyon, France. Conversation at the center with mobile fund-raising team. July 1976.

"People see that we just keep on going. Even after all the persecution, we are still praying, even more."

"By giving us the *Divine Principle,* Reverend Moon shows

us the way to come closer to God. That's why we follow him and why he can change the world."

"I always say that he is a man of God, a man through whom we can feel that God is working. He is someone who is continuing the message of Christ."

Just before leaving France, we went to the training center outside of Paris, near Versailles, where a fairly large group from the French church were gathered together for a family evening. We observed their tradition of home entertainment by members and had some chance for discussion, but the group was a little large for easy exchange. It was amateur talent night.

Paris. French church leaders. July 1976.

"We can overcome evil. We know the origin of evil."

"I begin to feel in my heart the God-love experience. It changed me completely. I discovered how to practice in a practical way in everyday life the love of God for others and to cut down the influence of evil."

"I can only witness for myself: When I began to study the *Divine Principle*, I felt God's love as really as my father, loving me since eternity."

"We are soldiers for a great revolution, the coming of a new age, one world under God, with God living in our heart, in our home, in our society, in our nation. We are living in a time when we have to unite spiritual and physical life, that is, religion, politics, economics, culture, artistic expression, et cetera."

England

Arriving in London, we went first to the fashionable downtown-area flat that is the headquarters of the Unification Church in England. After a brief introduction to those members present in the London center, we left almost immediately for "the farm." This farm property was given to the church by a couple who are somewhat older than the usual new member. They had, in fact, come to know the

Italian-born Luigi enjoys work at a Unification Church farm in England.

church through their daughter. Subsequently, they joined, but then the daughter left the church. In the course of this process they gave the Unification family their farm. It was in need of reconstruction, and the members who occupy it are in process of rebuilding it. Although it is an active and productive farm, it serves also as the training center. Those who come out for instruction do some work in addition to listening to lectures while there. (The director is not really happy until each guest gets a little manure on his shoes.) After a meal with the working members of the farm, we drove to a house the church has bought to turn into an elementary school. Their aim is to rear their own children—and those who would like the same atmosphere—in a Christian setting.

From there we drove to another farm. This is not a productive farm but a house in the country that is the family's activity headquarters. Here we saw the printing press for their fund-raising enterprises. They print cards and brochures for sale, as well as their own newspapers and literature. This also is the center for the mobile missionary teams that travel out into various parts of England. That evening we had dinner with the entire assembled crew, perhaps thirty or forty people. As is usual, they begin each gathering by singing, which in this case took on the character of the Scots, the Irish, and the Welsh. After dinner we began a long interview session of questions and answers with those present at the table. The movement in England seems to be flourishing, although not as vigorously as that in Germany and perhaps not as much as in France.

A farm outside London, Conversation with English members. July 1976.

"What first attracted me was the kind of people I met. They started talking to me about God and the heart of God. They were very sincere, very dedicated."

"I have always been a great believer in God, but I could not find him in the established church."

"It changed me. You better believe it. I used to spend most of my time drunk."

"I found a sense of freedom. I thought before I was free, but I realize now I was not free, that I was held in by my selfishness."

"Reverend Moon has taught us that if the Unification Church does not build the kingdom of heaven, God will begin another church."

"It is a privilege to be in the movement. It has nothing to do with compulsion. I refuse to think you can ever build the kingdom of heaven with any form of compulsion. You can't. It must be done voluntarily."

"How does the spirit of God control the world? He wants to control the world with love. To control the world with heavenly principles is not a fearsome thing but a very beautiful thing."

"It must be a shock to parents to see such a change come about in their son. For me, the Principle really showed me God, intellectually as well as emotionally. Then I changed my life so much that I came to a complete breakdown with my parents. I was to dedicate my life to the world, not just to my family. This creates conflict in families. You love your family very much, but the whole world is your family now."

"I think if people really get to love each other as brothers and sisters in the right way, and really express their hearts, people will feel this and send it on."

"Reverend Moon is part of God's work in restoring man. Because the situation is right in the world today, God wants to use a person as a central focus for his love. I see Reverend Moon as being used in that way."

"If you experience the love of God you certainly cannot run away from it. I did not join the church because I wanted to. I felt I had no choice, because I had experienced the love of God in such a way that I knew I could not live without it. And that feeling grows."

The Netherlands

When we arrived in Amsterdam, we first went to the town church center and discovered that the activities in Holland are neither extensive nor the membership wide. Some of the Dutch members are on detached service to other countries. We proceeded almost immediately to the training center outside Amsterdam, on the coast (Bergen an Zee). Given the youth population that streams in through the train station to visit Amsterdam each day, this center attracts an international student body. A small training session was in progress, which included students from many countries. Here again we had dinner and were able to interview both those who had come for the training session and also those older members of the church involved in operating the center.

We learned that Holland is not an easy mission country. The Dutch are too reserved, they say, when it comes to accepting public approach to discuss religion. But those who do join are stalwart members, who often go out to other countries as missionaries.

Amsterdam. Conversation with Dutch church members. July 1976.

"Your love for God must be stronger than love for yourself. This is what the *Divine Principle* teaches."

"Unification doctrine is restored Christianity. It is actually Christianity in its maturity."

Germany

On the short trip to Germany, I went first to the Frankfurt building that serves as headquarters for the extensive list of church centers operated all through the country. However, the main teaching operations in Germany are located in two training centers, one outside Munich and one outside

PHOTO BY AUTHOR

PHOTO BY BRACEY HOLT

Left: Training center in Germany. *Right:* German publications.

Frankfurt, both of which I visited. Actual training programs were in session, and I spoke with the young people who had come out for training at the centers.

Volkswagen buses are used by the church all over Europe, but in Germany we sped down the autobahn (no speed limit) at speeds up to two hundred kilometers an hour in a black Mercedes. Along with the United States and Japan, Germany is the most vigorous and most successful mission country, in numbers and in finances. The mission teams being sent out to other countries now are trios of one Japanese, one American, and one German member. Clearly, Germany is the center of the mission movement in Europe.

37

Germany. Conversation with leaders at the training center outside Frankfurt. August 1976.

"We are like the Hitler Youth movement in the very intense idealism that we share. A complete commitment to the cause is another similarity. We feel an intense loyalty toward our leader. But the analogy is not fair, because the idealism that motivates this movement is different from Naziism because it is a religious idealism."

"Actually, we are willing to sacrifice ourselves, not for Reverend Moon as a person but for all mankind, for the ideals we are working for."

"If a leader in the Unification Church would do something that was contrary to the *Divine Principle*, I certainly would not follow his example."

"I have complete trust and faith in Reverend Moon, and I am confident that he would not ask me to do anything immoral."

"The main thing in the movement is not that we are all drawn to Reverend Moon as a person but more that we are drawn to what he is saying and what he does."

"I think many people compare us with the Hitler Youth because the discipline in our movement is something rarely found in other movements."

"Brainwashing is a hilarious charge. It is spiritual rebirth or reeducation in a positive way. Today, so few people are seeking this that they cannot believe it can occur."

"People need sensation. Newspapers could not feed people by just telling them that there is this group that has a nice experience with God and that these people are trying to better themselves and the world. People would not buy the newspapers."

"I know how committed we are. We all work 100 percent to make this ideal a reality. It is a great temptation to tell a person a white lie in order that he will give you a small donation. But no one here can justify this kind of behavior. This is absolutely wrong and we condemn it."

"All of us have had some wonderful experience with fund raising. We are giving something to the people."

"We are not simply a religious movement. We are a movement to reform our society at many levels. We work through organizations to have some kind of impact on reform of education, reform of economic system, to have some kind of effect in politics. If we work with sincerity and clarity of purpose, this is not a 'front.'"

"We are not supportive of any ideology of any nation. The ideas of the Unification Church are to make one unified mankind, to make a great family, to help people have more respect and love for each other."

"No, I don't feel dependent on Reverend Moon. But I feel dependent upon God, and I find that the *Divine Principle* is a direction for life."

"I personally do feel a little dependent on Reverend Moon. He brought me to God. And it is thanks to him that I could experience God and that I have come to a deeper relationship with people than I ever had before."

"For one thing, I don't pray to Reverend Moon. I never have. This is ridiculous."

"We talk in the family about many things you don't hear on the outside. We talk about the spiritual world, and to most people this is completely foreign."

"We are trying to achieve unity in this organization. And not an external unity like you have in a military organization but an internal unity of heart."

"I think the ideal will last forever. Even though Reverend Moon has to die once like everyone else, his ideal will continue."

"God has a deadline for the restoration of the earth, and we believe the cycle has come to the point where the world is ready to change."

"We expect to have very significant results by 1981, but if in fact the dispensation is to be extended to the year 2000, it will make life more difficult for me. I will have to make more sacrifices. But I am in the movement for the long run, and this does not bother me at all."

39

"I don't think it is necessary to convert millions of people, just a handful."

Munich, Germany. Conversation at the church center. August 1976.

"I was impressed by how free they were and how much happier they were than I was. I found that only a selfless way of living can do away with all these problems."

"It is very difficult for people to understand why God suddenly calls the movement into being. People throw us in with a bunch of other religious groups and see all religious groups the same way."

"It was more the relationship between me and my parents that was at fault. The inner part I never discussed with my parents. I really never discussed what I felt about these things. It was a great shock to them when I joined, and they had a violent reaction."

Italy

Because I had previously spent a year in Rome, teaching for the Benedictines, I looked forward to my visit to Italy. Milano is the Unification Church headquarters in Italy, but we left immediately for the training center on Lake Como, where a weekend session was in progress. The Italian church family appears more relaxed and has less trouble with the parents of members. Several sets of parents were at

PHOTO BY AUTHOR

PHOTO BY BRACEY HOLT

Left: Italian publications. *Right:* Training center in Italy.

the center over the weekend. They seemed less ready to quarrel over the doctrine as long as they liked the people with whom their children were now involved. It was interesting for a straitlaced American to discover that Catholicism in Italy is able to react to Moonies with a much greater tolerance than we might imagine. The Marxist political left and financial chaos are the absorbing topics in Italy today. Moonies are simply one among many unrecognized groups springing up and being tolerated.

Lake Como, Italy. Conversation at weekend training center. August 1976.

"I always desired to live in a community. And I could see these people were realizing their ideals completely."

"Our movement desires the unification of all churches, and this is what I like very much. Also the dynamic of this movement. What is said is done."

"When I met Reverend Moon I saw that the Principles were his life. He didn't just talk about the Principle, but he put it into practice. He struck me as a man of faith and especially as a man of love. One particular thing that struck me very much was that this Korean fellow was so appreciated by the Japanese people."

"What he says with strength in public is the same message he will give with love individually."

"I see a relationship between Reverend Moon and Christ because they both took responsibility for the world."

"Each nation has its own peculiarities in practicing the Principles. The Principles are the same, but the Italians, for example, developed more the aspect of feeling, of the heart. French people will develop more the spiritual aspect; Germans will develop more the rational aspect."

"I don't think we will be the ones that will realize the kingdom of heaven, but I think God will realize the kingdom of heaven through us."

"I was struck by the brotherhood among the members, seeing how different they were from the young people outside. They were so different that I thought it was a dream. I am living the biggest ideal one can find in the world."

"Yes, we have people who come with a psychological mental weakness. Because of their mental state they cause problems during the course."

"We are trying to improve their personality and push them to express their love toward others, work for others. If they don't give love, they can't receive it."

"I don't think we live in a miserable way. This is the way we choose to live freely."

"Compared with what he [Reverend Moon] did for us, I feel that, with doing what I do, I give him a gift."

Denmark

My last visit took us to Copenhagen for two weeks. The Danish family is quite small but also quite vigorous, which seems to be the case in all the Scandinavian countries. The movement is not large in number and not immensely successful financially but nevertheless stable and established. We were to spend two weeks with a friend in

PHOTO BY AUTHOR

Erika Zamberger (second from left), head of Danish church family, answers questions at a street information center in Copenhagen.

Copenhagen and so had a chance to get to know that small church family more casually. Mission work is hard in Scandinavia, and even the newspapers dismiss the movement as unimportant because it is so small.

Copenhagen. Conversation with members at Danish family center. August 1976.

"It is not just theory. You can practice what you believe in, and that is very important. But you can't do it alone, and therefore we have to be here with other people to do it together."

"If this is the truth, then the future will show it, but we know for sure we are building the foundation."

"Reverend Moon teaches us we have to sacrifice. We are willing to give our lives for God, not just go to church on Sunday for one hour. But if we work hard, we can overcome; we can do it. It won't be easy, but we really can."

Austria

I was not able to visit Austria, but I caught up with their leader in America. The story is one of suppression. The Unification Church has now been legally outlawed in Austria.

Washington, D.C. Interview with Austrian church leader. November 1976.

"Legally we do not exist. We are really now an underground organization. On a private level you can do a lot of things which you could never do as an organization. If you ask me about the situation I can only say that I love it. . . .
"I once said to my people that there is one thing I am afraid of. That is when the time of our suffering will be over. I think the fighting group should be kept small. . . .
"I came from an average Christian family, which means we went to church every year at Christmas, providing it was not raining."

What Do the People Say in the United States?

Children of the world unite!
Together we must change the wrong to right.

—from a Unification Church song

My wife and I returned from Europe in early September and prepared for the long-planned trip to Korea and Japan. But along came a telephone call from Unification headquarters asking if I could come back to the East Coast first, to participate as an observer at the impending Washington Monument rally, Moon's last public appearance in the United States. I agreed to go, little realizing the real significance of the rally in church members' minds or the fact that members and leaders from all over the world would be gathered in Washington. The occasion provided an interviewer's field day, but we had to compromise the travel plan by asking my son to go out to Japan ahead of me to start there. I then flew out to join him the day the rally ended.

On the afternoon of the Washington Monument rally and Reverend Moon's address, I was talking to two young Moonies who were handing out advertisements on the rally. As I talked with them about their background and how they came to join the church, two boys came out of the Monument and asked me to move my briefcase, which was beside the bicycles they were unchaining. An exchange ensued, and one of them looked up at me as he was bent over working on the bike lock and said, "You a Moonie?" to which I replied, "No." "Well," he said, looking up again, "you look like one." And so I did, with my relatively short hair and a plain dark gray travel suit. It was also not the last time people would look at me suspiciously as if they were sure, because I traveled in church circles, that I had lost my reason and become a Moonie in fact as well as in appearance.

To understand Moon in America and all the uproar in the press, one first must realize that the church claims only four to six thousand full-time members in the United States, with perhaps another four thousand part-time (the church moves too fast to keep very accurate records). Whenever I spoke to audiences about the Moon movement and asked them to guess the church size in America, I inevitably got responses that estimated the size at about ten times what officials claim. It is fascinating, isn't it, to think of the impact such a small group has been able to create?

The Washington Monument rally gave me an opportunity to meet and interview some of the world church leaders. If you are outside the church and lack some understanding of its doctrine, I discovered, it is almost impossible to understand the city speaking tours Sun Myung Moon planned for all the fifty states, or the Madison Square Garden, Yankee Stadium, and finally Washington Monument rallies. Only in a minor sense are these public-relations ventures and evangelical campaigns. To compare them with Billy Graham's crusades is to miss their significance. Without going into great detail, they are seen as providential events, carefully timed, which must be acted out if the church's mission is to be fulfilled. They are "vertical proclamations" to which the multitude is witness.

As the newspapers reported, the earlier Yankee Stadium rally was not a success. However, it was not a failure in the usual sense of the term. In Unification doctrine, to undergo adversity is a necessity for a future growth. The rainstorm that destroyed their decorations and cut down the crowd, plus the hostility and disturbances both inside and outside the stadium, served only to whip up the members to redouble their effort next time. The Washington Monument rally fulfilled their conditions and in their eyes was a

45

Top: Madison Square Garden rally, September 18, 1974. Twenty thousand showed up, but many left early. *Left:* Moonie street witness urges a New Yorker to attend the Yankee Stadium rally. *Right:* Young Moonie works hard to promote Yankee Stadium rally.

Top: A severe rainstorm ruined decorations and cut down the crowd at Yankee Stadium. *Left:* A cleanup-crew member takes time to play with a new friend. The Moonies removed all, or almost all, of their promotion posters during the night following the Yankee Stadium rally. *Right:* Sun Myung Moon and his translator, Bo Hi Pak, greet the crowd at Yankee Stadium. In Unification thought, this adversity was a necessary prelude to further growth and redoubled efforts.

UC/NFP

Top: A view of the rally from the top of the Washington Monument. *Center:* Members of the Korean Folk Ballet help drum up enthusiasm at the Washington Monument rally. They perform at many of the public events sponsored by the Unification Church. *Left:* The Washington Monument rally helped fulfill the divine timetable. *Right:* Nei Salonen (president of the American Unification Church) and his wife lead followers to Washington as part of the campaign to heal the Watergate fracture.

success, even though most people came to enjoy the music and the world's largest fireworks display. After all, the aim was not mass conversion but the fulfillment of a divine timetable.

Washington, D.C. Conversation at the church center with an early missionary from Korea to America. September 1976.

"Great leaders, and also ordinary leaders, like Reverend Moon, speak differently according to the situation. . . . Reverend Moon's work can be interpreted differently by different people, based on their own religious background and their intellectual understanding. . . . Reverend Moon is one of the potential messiahs, because his role has to be fulfilled, and it is not yet fulfilled. So I don't say he is the actual messiah. Whether he will be the one I can't say yet. . . . Reverend Moon indicated very clearly that he learned from other people. Not all the *Divine Principle* came through his received revelation. . . .

"Before I joined [1954], the lecture was very simple. The new members with different backgrounds joined and shared what they found from their study and what they thought and felt. So this long book came out, but in the beginning it was very simple. . . .

"I saw a great light in the *Divine Principle* and in some points very much similarity between Swedenborg and Reverend Moon's teachings. . . . I don't know what attracted me. Externally, he was not interesting. Externally, the group were insignificant people; none were trained theologians. But I just perceived a sense of a deep spiritual atmosphere in which I felt at home. Through my spiritual experience I know where God has come closer. . . . I thought: How could these things happen in Korea? But my disillusion with European Christianity helped me to realize that if God chose a small country like Judea to send Jesus, why not Korea? Why couldn't Korea be chosen? . . .

"We do not make a specific effort to create a warm atmosphere. Each one who joins experiences great joy and a great feeling of hope. That makes each one happy. When happy ones gather, the atmosphere is happy and warm. . . .

"Reverend Moon will learn, or he will receive further revelations as he goes along. Then I suspect his view may be changed, but as long as Communism is anti-God, he will be in the other camp. . . .

"To be effective in your work or in fulfilling God's will,

Daphne Greene, an outspoken and articulate opponent of the Unification Church. Her daughter was still a member at the time of this writing. (Editor's note: Representatives of the Tucson deprogramming center and Rabbi Davis were invited to submit photographs. Michael E. Trausht, a lawyer representing the Freedom of Thought Foundation in Tucson, responded with the foundation's refusal. Rabbi Davis did not respond.)

Reverend Moon said from the beginning we better bring in leadership, influential people, into our movement. He would always like to join hands with leaders. To make this world physically a better world, how can you separate religion completely from politics?"

After returning home from Europe, my attention turned to the movement's active opposition. The intelligence reports are as intense in the antichurch network as they are within the church. Almost everywhere I went or wrote, I found that the word of my project had preceded me, usually with the negative connotation that I was "unsafe." Translated, this meant that I had made no prior commitment to destroy or to expose the church. I had visited the anti-Moon vigil at the Lincoln Monument the night before the September Moon rally in Washington and picked up some antichurch contacts. I had gone to White Plains, New York, to see Rabbi Maurice Davis, one of the early opposition, and gained addresses of the antichurch organization. Once home in California, I spent the better part of one day with Daphne Greene near San Francisco. She is a well-informed opponent who took on a battle against the church as her personal mission after two of her children joined. (One daughter is still a member; the son is now out. I interviewed both. The San Francisco newspapers reported the family's attempt to kidnap and deprogram the daughter, her injury in the process of a struggle, hospitalization, and her eventual return to the church.)

Through these contacts I gained a mountain of literature and interviews with deprogrammers and ex-members. These people ranged in attitude from vowing to destroy the church to being neutral to looking back on their active days with longing. One absolute conclusion I have reached is that there is no universal opinion or reaction from either those inside or those outside. To pretend that there is, oversimplifies an immensely complex situation.

I had decided that I should go through a regular teaching-training program myself and chose the Northern California center both for its proximity and its notoriety. I began by having dinner with the young people invited to the San Francisco, Washington Street, center—while the pickets marched outside. After dinner and the introductory

PHOTO BY AUTHOR

Lecture and lunch at the Boonville training center north of San Francisco.

talk, those of us who were going on departed for the Boonville training center, which is north of San Francisco, near the Mendocino coast. My hostess that night was a girl later taken from the church under a conservatorship and deprogrammed at the Tucson center. We have since met on a Chicago TV program and exchanged letters about her experiences.

Activities began rather late on Saturday morning, since people had been arriving at all hours on Friday night. The format is simple: You are placed in small sections with a group leader, with whom you stay for the whole time. One active member is assigned to each invited guest; there is exercise in the morning, organized games in the afternoon, spirited singing led by a mild rock combo to start off every session. The gospel singing is lively, but there is little really to distinguish the program from the Baptist church mountain camp I frequented as a child, the emotional aim of which was quite similar. The core of the session is a series of lectures setting forth the basic teaching of the Principle.

I wanted to visit Boonville because it is most often mentioned in negative accounts, since the introductory sessions do not mention the church or Reverend Moon. The reason for this, I was told, is connected to the situation of the sixties around Berkeley. Because of the hostility at that time, a separate foundation was established, Creative Community Projects. Boonville is legally the property of that foundation. As far as I can tell, Boonville is special—every other training center identifies its connection to the Unification movement—but Boonville's reticence gives rise to the charge that people are lured to the centers deceptively.

Recently the San Francisco Unification center has been continually in the news. The headline event has been the trial considering parents' requests for conservatorships for and deprogramming of five Moonies over the age of twenty-one. The lower court, with more immediate sympathy to the pleas of the parents, granted the conservatorships. The decision was reversed by a higher court review, although at the time this book went to press the case was still under appeal. The constitutional issues at stake are significant, but the interesting point for this study is the whole question of the special quality of the San Francisco group.

Four of the five involved in this case defected from the church, which indicates the vulnerability of the San Francisco community. As noted, Reverend Moon is not at first mentioned to those approached by the group, and the commitment solicited is one to a set of educational and cultural goals. This sounds inviting at first, but when the chips are down, if there is no allegiance to the religious and spiritual life and the theological perspective, it is easier to abandon conviction when evidence comes out against the church. When one is encouraged to do one's own thing rather than to sacrifice oneself for a higher goal, allegiance is easily broken as soon as the course of events does not suit the individual. Apparently, indirect, or "soft," indoctrination is not lasting. Either one faces and accepts Moon's teaching and life-style or one's dedication is temporary and lacks depth.

San Francisco Bay area. Conversation with antichurch leader. October 1976.

"If I really thought it was up to me to take responsibility from creation on and to save us from negative evil, I would be a wreck. It is a guilt trip. That's why the ones who do leave, just run; they split. . . . It is a satanic, negative theory that is being worshiped, and the soul of the human being is just stepped on."

San Francisco. Interview at church center with a member. October 1976.

"With all the kidnappings, it is difficult for all the kids here to have full trust in their parents. I feel that I have a deeper commitment to God than having a nice afternoon at home. . . .

"I love fund raising, selling flowers in the streets. I have learned so much from fund raising, to be just humble and still when people are yelling at you. . . . I don't know of anything going on here as far as people being pressured to give funds. I only know of people giving money because

53

they think it is for a larger purpose than owning it themselves. . . .

"I feel changed. It is gradual. I have developed humility and a listening ability. I used to be really critical of people. I don't think there is any radical change, at least not that would frighten anyone. I have much more of an inner peace. . .

"In so many families, there is already a breakdown before they come here. Then this works like a catalyst. But if a parent really loves his kid, he should come here and find out why he is doing it. . . .

"When I heard the Principle I just hit the ceiling in excitement. It really made sense. Of course, the thing that is so exciting about the Principle is that it is not just an intellectual thing. The more you work, the more you give to other people, the deeper the insight. You can hear the same lecture over and over. The more you actualize it, the deeper your relationship to God is, the more you understand."

San Francisco. Interview at the church center with a leader. October 1976.

"We try to encourage people's activity. Less than 1 percent of the people connected with our foundation [Creative Community Projects] are actually involved in full-time flower selling. . . .

"I grew up in an orthodox Jewish household in New York. I myself had difficulty establishing a true relationship with God, although I desired to do that. . . . All this stuff about brainwashing is ironic. Because, from my experience, this life is the most challenging, most responsible, most incredible kind of existential burden. . . .

"About 1 percent of the people who are involved with a community [Creative Community Projects Foundation] project go on to be involved with the Unification Church. We talk about it, but we don't force it on people. . . .

"What I see myself living is the fulfillment of my Jewish heritage, a covenant relationship. I am trying to make religious people understand what it is to bind together in a world that reflects God's ideal, and God's covenant."

Claremont, California. Interview with ex–church member. October 1976.

"The original thing that influenced me to look deeper was the concept of God suffering for us. . . . I had always been independent, always been able to do just what I pleased.

But you give that up for value. I didn't feel that I was tricked into giving that up. I felt I was giving up something but that I received something. . . . I might join again. I'm not negative. I'm just saying right now that I don't know whether it is the right place to be or the wrong place to be."

Claremont, California. Interview with ex-Moonie who left voluntarily. November 1976.

"My feelings are very mixed. I still believe in the church very much; if I had to do it over again I would not do, I think, what I did do [i.e., leave]. . . . I saw a lot of the top people, and I have no doubts at all that all are very clearly dedicated. I am sure that they are not in any way in for personal gain. There was nothing about my inside experience that disillusioned me. . . .

"I worked so hard and there was nothing left. I felt so empty I didn't care anymore. Everybody has his own limit of how much he can endure. I reached mine not because I was asked to but because I did it on my own. On my part it was voluntary. Nobody ever pushed me. . . .

"What causes people to leave? The people that I have observed I think are disillusioned. And a lot of people [leave] because they are not willing to work as hard as they should and as hard as requested. . . .

"I think if I had to do it all over again, I am sure I would have found the strength to hang on and stay in. They don't tie you up and prevent you from leaving. And if you decide to go out, you are certainly welcome to go."

Claremont, California. Interview with ex-member, kidnapped and forcibly deprogrammed, now involved in deprogramming others. November 1976.

"It is a frightening experience to go through. To have everything that you think is yourself that could never be changed—your values, your loyalties, your standards—to see them all completely altered. It is a shocking experience. I guess it is like a nervous breakdown. And there is an area where I am afraid to probe by myself because I know I can't trust myself. . . .

"In a way it [life in the church] was a wonderful experience. Because of the closeness of the people and the cooperation and having a purpose in life. There is so much enthusiasm and consideration. So there were some things about it that were enjoyable and good, and this was a genuine part. There is so much hope, and you can feel that.

Left: Students discuss a difficult concept. *Right:* Unification Theological Seminary, Barrytown, New York.

You really feel that you are accomplishing something I guess. There is a tremendous satisfaction in every day. . . .

"I don't think you can deprogram someone on their terms. They have to feel cornered. . . . We always watched people around the seventh month. It hits you every time, and you want to get out. I would many, many times just sit and cry because I wanted to leave and I could not. . . .

"You come to believe so much that God is depending on you and that the fate of the world is on your shoulders, and everything depends on every decision you make. The last thing you want to do is to fail."

I went East for my interview visit to the church's Barrytown, New York, seminary en route to a conference in Washington, D.C., and a Pomona College alumni meeting in Boston. On the academic side, I met with students selected by the Moon hierarchy to go on to graduate schools. On the mystery-thriller side, I heard the story of the group who had been kidnapped by paid professionals and deprogrammed but had escaped and returned to the church. The drama and emotion involved in these captures and escapes put Wild-West movies to shame. The heartbreaking quality of the family confrontations are beyond the dreams of soap-opera scriptwriters. Next, I interviewed the remaining church leaders whom I had not yet contacted. Then I asked to hear and observe Reverend Moon speak to his followers. I had read all the available church literature and had read *Master Speaks* transcriptions of his talks by the dozens, but I wanted to witness the event myself. The response was not to invite me to a Sunday service, when he usually speaks, but to ask me to be a guest for Children's Day, one of the church's four official holidays.

When I arrived, the Belvedere estate (Tarrytown, New York) was awash with people, and I was ushered in late, after the conclusion of a ceremony to be witnessed by church members only. Reverend Moon had begun speaking, and Colonel Pak was translating. The talk, largely an exposition of Old Testament biblical themes from his own special perspective, went on for over two hours and might have run four to six hours. The setting for these gatherings is the former garage on the estate, now transformed into a meeting room with a tent erected to extend the space in order to pack in two thousand or so. Contrary to what one might expect, it is not overtly a very emotionally charged scene, but actually rather friendly and family-like.

UC/NFP   UC/NFP

Belvedere Estate, Tarrytown, New York.

Tarrytown, New York. Interview with American church leader. November 1976.

"Our members are overzealous because they are young. I remember the first couple of people I witnessed to. I really tried to strong-arm them. And nobody called it brainwashing because that was not a factor. I had such a conviction that the most important thing for them to do was to see things this way, my liberating them. . . . We certainly believe that the closest that you can come to knowing what

God's desire is for our life is by working with Reverend Moon. We believe that he is such a direct channel. And that is what I felt. . . .

"Renewal is in order constantly. But in our church the radicalism is at the very center. It is Reverend Moon who is forever upsetting the apple cart. . . .

"The movement in Korea was the formation stage, and the movement in Japan was growth stage, and the movement in America was meant to be the perfection stage. . . . I don't think the real church in America has emerged at all. This is my own faith that the American church and the tradition of the American church will begin from now. Now as he [Reverend Moon] moves on to other missions I think the real tradition of the American church will emerge. . . .

"Late 1972 is when the fund raising really began. Belvedere became our first project. It was simply more money than we ever could hope to raise. We stopped everything we were doing and went out to raise money. And that was a revolutionary concept, and it was a crisis of faith. We felt we couldn't do it, but we felt we must do it. Therefore we did it. . . . Now it is so difficult for people in some places to go fund raising for the Unification Church. So there is an incredible pressure on them in order to fulfill a certain goal, and yet at the same time the temptation to mislead, or to be deliberately vague about what they are doing, is incredible. And I don't approve of it, and I know Reverend Moon does not approve. . . .

"I feel, and I am pretty sure that Reverend Moon feels the same, that a lot of the publicity about the church will die down quite a bit within the next six months, and yet the church will be burrowing its way into the fabric of America more deeply, to reemerge at a later point as a substantial and permanent institution. . . .

"The healthiest thing in our church is the feeling that he inspires in everyone to want to keep up right with him. He is the pacesetter. . . .

"Members of our church who had Jewish background had a longing for something that was no longer vital within their tradition and yet was there and ready to be reawakened. . . .

"In the next generation we will emphasize educating our children."

New York City. Conversation at the Unification Church's national headquarters with public relations officials and selected members. September 1976.

"There is more commitment now on our part to explain to people what we are doing. Four years ago that didn't exist."

"With all the publicity and growth of the movement, parents no longer take the word of their son or daughter but take the word from the media."

"Families who had various tensions, emotional problems, severely possessive in relationships with each other—these families had a very difficult time when their children joined the church. It seemed to be a catalyst for the surfacing of all the problems, and it became a scapegoat. The church was accused of all the problems between the parents and the child, whereas with or without the church there was a problem there."

"We assure our parents: I love you a lot, but I have a cause which is larger than our family. Can you understand this and can you let me go and do what I feel is right?"

"Many members who join, stay, but some are just carried away at first and then later think it over and say, 'This is too hard for me, I don't want to go a way that requires this much commitment.' Then they will drop out and have to pick up the pieces of their previous life."

"I wanted to be a nurse. My parents saw a drastic change from somebody who was a college student and then decided to drop out in two weeks. That showed them I had changed so much somehow, they just assumed that something was wrong with my mind."

"Being a member of the church requires that you deny yourself something you wanted before. There is somewhere in all our minds a part that wants to believe that the church is a fake. If we return to being self-centered, the mind has to justify itself because there is guilt because we left."

"What kidnapping did to me personally was not terribly damaging, but what it did to my family I think would be the damaging part. I feel that I can't trust them anymore. My trust in my family is really gone, and I was close to my family. That is really a tragedy."

"I have been in the church ten years, and many times I have thought, I don't know, maybe I should go to Florida and get

North American publications.

a nice apartment and a color TV. If I ever left the church I would have to say in all honesty the reason would be that I am not willing to sacrifice, I am not willing to go the hard road any more. I just want to give up and live for myself a little bit."

"Ex-members are highly idealistic. They responded to this kind of call. And their only way out is to say the cause is at fault to prevent admitting they are copping out."

"Ninety-nine percent of those who leave have a friendly feeling toward the church. Becoming antichurch is a defense against becoming church, the defense against a feeling that they have deserted a good cause."

"When they are deprogrammed, there is a family waiting for them, a family of deprogrammed members, anti-Moon people. And actually they are drawn to each other in the same way we are, by a common purpose and belief."

Boston area. Interview with psychiatrist who has treated members and ex-members. November 1976.

"It is relatively easy to learn to control almost completely the behavior and the thinking, the attitude, the mind, and the destiny of another person. . . .

"Their attitude is nonhumanistic, that is to say that the individual and his special world view is not important. There is no particular, real concern for the idiosyncratic, individualistic qualities of the other human being. . . .

"The first thing the parents see is when the kids come, they are not the same. They don't quite look at them, the language is different, they don't talk in as complicated vocabulary, they are humorless, basically humorless. . . . From that time on the individual is in the state of thought control. You might say also that I think the emotional and intellectual growth stops at that point. What I am describing is a rapid and catastrophic change of mental states, of mental functioning. On the way in and out of this kind of state there is a high vulnerability to breakdown. . . .

"Moonies tend to be young students, bright, and fairly straight. . . .

"I also think that a free society takes risks, mental health risks, by allowing people to be free."

Washington, D.C. Interview with early California convert, now a church official. November 1976.

"I became increasingly interested in the idea of changing and transforming myself. I could not do that as long as I was self-centered and basically materialistic. . . . I was immediately impressed with the whole atmosphere of the place. There was just something different about the quality of the life. A sense of unity and love and harmony. . . .

"I think he [Moon] always has this burning desire, but I think he is very careful about how he lets it out when he meets somebody for the first time, be it a nation, a group, or a person. He is a man of tremendous will and determination. I think his purpose has been unwavering. I think he reveals it more now. . . .

"I am sure that the leadership of the church will be judged by its fruits before God as everyone is judged. What I see in the church is that the church is moving people toward God and toward a higher standard. But the church is not perfect. . . .

"I think religions are not supposed to be losers. I think it is the biggest myth of Christianity that you had to get nailed to the cross to be saved. I think the fear of success or running from success is stupid. So success doesn't corrupt. Satan corrupts. There is a difference. Material things and power and anything can be used for a good purpose and can be used for an evil purpose. . . .

"I have committed myself to this whole thing, while recognizing that there were dangers. Everybody has to make a choice about how they can do the best thing. I have to think of this. Is what I am doing the most effective thing? And I will be asking myself that question my whole life. . . .

"I think in 1981 there will be an increasing expansion of our foundations, spiritually and physically. But to what extent I don't know. . . . What I can relate to personally and what I am going through is that the impact from him on me—his ideas, his personality, his feelings, et cetera —has been a very transforming thing. I think God is working through Reverend Moon, and I think he is the central person through whom He works today. I think that Reverend Moon has conquered sin. I think the man has a state of spiritual purity that I think no one else can claim in the past. I think he has that kind of status. I think the world will be saved. I don't think it will be completely saved in Reverend Moon's lifetime."

Washington, D.C. Interview with an American center director. November 1976.

"In the beginning of the movement you had to be very strong spiritually. I feel that spiritual experience was much stronger in the early days. We didn't have fund raising in the early days. The drop-out rate was very high, much higher than now. Life in the centers was not yet very organized. The formal center was started much later. . . .

"Until just recently we have had no problems with the parents. But when Reverend Moon came to America, he said there was an urgency and work to be done, so many people were pulled out of school to participate in the restoration. That changed the whole thing. . . . Young people sometimes don't know how to handle problems with parents wisely.

"One thing people don't understand is that we are functioning in a time of emergency."

Washington, D.C. Interview with American member. November 1976.

"I have found God as a reality. I have felt God working through me. I am just trying to place myself more fully at his disposal, to be an instrument, to demonstrate the truth of the Principle. . . . I believe that he [Moon] is my spiritual father. The Principle is very basic. You live for others and God will be with you. If you give love, more will come back. But you have to give first. . . .

"He is trying to bless us and bring us into perfection as individuals and as families. And the process is under way, and it is an irreversible process."

"The idea of True Parents is a necessary symbol to bring mankind to the consciousness of being one family. As a True Parent, he is the father you never had; he is the father I never had. We have to get back to kindergarten and spiritually learn the language and meaning of the heart. . . .

"I think that our beginning point was a far greater distance than from now to fulfillment."

Washington, D.C. Interview with an early leader in the American church. November 1976.

"I look forward to the termination of fund raisings. Unfortunate but necessary—what we are doing. It is psychologically difficult for many people, but other people have tremendous experiences. I think the message from headquarters is that if they are asked if they are from the Unification Church, then to identify that it is, but not to volunteer it. I think initially anyway, especially probably among younger leaders, they felt very O.K. about being deceptive. So I think we learned a lesson, I hope we did. . . .

"The church has not . . . encouraged members to go home frequently. Younger members get the impression that it is wrong, that it is something they should not want to do. . . .

"There is no regular counseling for people with problems; however, people sometimes don't have the courage to share the problems they have with their own faith with someone outside that faith."

Journey to Tucson

If you look for the phenomena that capture all the puzzles of the Moon movement in the most graphic illustration, deprogramming and kidnapping surely lead the list. When you hear the stories about hired kidnappers, the escape and recapture of members, you say, "No, don't try out that script on Hollywood. They will never buy it." The Wild West has been reborn, replete with hideaways, intelligence operations, police assistance, and dramatic escapes and chase scenes. One aspect usually missing in Hollywood movies is that parents act as the co-conspirators in these episodes. These confrontations pit child against parent in emotion-laden scenes.

The question to be answered is: In a country built on religious freedom, where immigrants came to escape from religious persecution, can anyone justify seizing and then physically restraining an adult person in order to subject him to psychological bombardment until he recants? Have we not learned the lesson we fled across oceans to try to enshrine into law? Of course, those who engage in such vigilante tactics insist (1) that the young people (usually in their early twenties) are not in their right mind and have not made this religious decision freely, no matter what they protest; and (2) that the religious movement is ruled out as illegitimate in advance. Therefore, force to break it is authorized and involves no infringement of religious liberty.

What does kidnapping and deprogramming involve? Like many aspects of the Moon phenomenon, this question has no single answer. Some individuals who operate on an ad hoc basis call themselves deprogrammers. Rabbi Maurice Davis says he deprograms simply by having people come to his office and sit on the couch and talk with him. The really knotty problems involve the paid professionals who may charge five to ten thousand dollars to seize a child and put him or her through an elaborate ordeal. Sometimes sympathetic parents' homes are used for this process. At other times, as in the case of the Tucson Freedom of Thought Foundation, an elaborately prepared ranch is involved which maintains a security operation. Furthermore, deprogramming clearly involves no single technique. In addition to varying from person to person and situation to situation, it has undergone an increasing sophistication of the techniques employed.

Unification Church headquarters report about 206 kidnappings and forced deprogrammings since 1973. Twenty-five percent of these have involved legal conservatorships, but 50 percent of the total have come within the last year, the majority in the San Francisco Bay area. There seems to be some possibility that the person can ask for a writ of prohibition against the conservatorship in advance. Church officials report that previously about 50 percent of those forcibly deprogrammed returned to the church, but that, with improved, more sophisticated techniques and legal assistance, the percentage has dropped, at least as far as immediate return goes. One subtle psychological issue involved is to determine how much of any damage done is church-induced and how much results from the shock of the forced deprogramming itself. Psychiatrists report that the patient may experience "floating" (detachment from reality) for a period of up to a year and be unable to function normally and without assistance for that period.

Tucson's Freedom of Thought Foundation has recently become the most celebrated center for the deprogramming of Moonies, and I was anxious to visit it. Furthermore, in one of the uncanny switches surrounding this phenomenon, one of the deprogrammers at Tucson is a former seminary student whom I had met on my visit to the Unification center at Barrytown, and who had at that time voluntarily given me a long individual testimony on the merits of the Unification Church. I had also earlier met members at Boonville who are now deprogramming graduates. In general, the Tucson ranch claims to use legal and modern psychological techniques, which supports its image as a rehabilitation center. At the time of my efforts to visit, the *Los Angeles Times* had just done a front-page story on the center's activities (January 3, 1977). This put the center in the spotlight, and I met considerable resistance in trying to arrange my investigative visit.

The difficulty I had arranging a visit to the deprogramming/rehabilitation center caused it to be delayed until after my visit to the East. They kept postponing or canceling my dates. Thus, it happened that I had to go directly from my lengthy final interview with Reverend Moon to the night plane for Tucson. The ex-Moonie and present deprogrammer met me for breakfast and in fact stayed with me until my after-midnight departure. The trip was disappointing in the number of refused and canceled appointments, but it was still possible to touch a number of bases. Sometimes a refusal to discuss tells more than a direct conversation ever could. The Tucson center claims to be unique because of its openness and because it follows due legal process by using court-ordered conservatorships. Beneath these claims, however, lie some serious questions.

In the first place, repeated telephone calls to the Freedom of Thought Foundation Center by numerous intermediaries failed to produce the long-negotiated appointment with the directors, Joe and Esther Alexander. I decided to call myself and then go out. I did, but was refused on every hand. The reported openness of the center and its program was not extended to me. Young people who have left a cult certainly need a half-way house, and I could never deny that the Tucson center may fulfill a humanitarian service. What I encountered, however, was the same secretive, closed atmosphere of which they accuse the cults. It is an irony that the only place where I was denied admission in my eight months of travel around the globe was the Tucson center.

I spoke to the center's administrator in town, not at the center, to a Jewish rabbi and Protestant minister who are connected with the Center Advisory Board, to a lawyer who has handled a number of the legal cases involved, and to an ex-Moonie now living in town. All in all, in spite of the lack of openness, it was possible to get a fair idea of life back on the ranch in Tucson. In the first place, they make a clear point of saying that no deprogramming is done at the ranch itself. Only those who are undergoing rehabilitation after deprogramming are kept there. Of course, like the accusations made against the Moon movement of using multiple organizations manned by the same personnel, the Tucson center admits that the staff is involved in both operations. It is simply that the deprogramming is done away from the center, often in motels near where the individual is "snatched."

What happens? Through a Tucson lawyer, the parents who have been contacted by anti-Moon groups obtain a conservatorship through the courts in the county where the youth resides. Legal or not, the interesting fact is that these apprehensions are still conducted like kidnappings. The parents are usually involved as decoys to lure the child away from the church center. Then the apprehensions are swift and the individual removed to the prearranged deprogramming site with every possible speed. Why? To prevent resistance from church members and to keep the subject from attracting attention from police who might intervene. This forced, swift removal is the strange cloud that hangs over a supposedly legal action.

What is the issue concerning the use of conservatorships for this purpose? The legal problem is the question of whether the young person has a right to know in advance that a conservatorship is being sought. At present, deprogramming technique demands that this legal action be a strict secret until the sudden apprehension. The aim is to break the person before the period of the conservatorship is up or other legal means force the deprogrammers to produce the individual in public. This is quite different from confining a sick person to the local hospital. Should the "patient" have a right to protest before the conservatorship is granted and he is forcibly removed and kept in physical confinement and seclusion while he is worked on? If so, the court could then determine in advance whether conservatorship is warranted rather than after the person is deprogrammed.

The claim is made that only documented evidence that has been withheld from the church member is presented. However, when I asked to see the evidence of church misconduct, which I had searched the world over to uncover, I was told it could not be shared because it might let the church know what was being said and thus give them a chance to counter it with members in advance. Remember the situation in which the deprogrammers present facts for the church member's consideration: He has been decoyed and removed by physical restraint, and now he probably is in a motel room surrounded only by adversaries who admittedly are there until he recants. After he breaks down, he undergoes rehabilitation, again in a controlled atmosphere.

Of course, these tactics are what the deprogrammers claim the church uses in its prior conversion efforts. I found no evidence that that was so. Even if it were, one wonders if the cure is worse than the sickness? One supporter of the Tucson Center claims that those subjected to deprogramming should have no right of prior protest because "cancer has no legal right to be in the body." The medical analogy is misleading and also certainly involves an end-justifies-the-means mentality. Ironically, this is one of the chief accusations leveled against the Moon movement.

Has the subject first been deprived of his freedom by the religious group so that freedom of religion is not the issue? That seems difficult to determine, but surely it should be established legally *before* the subject is forcibly removed to undergo an intense and prolonged closed session from which he is not permitted exit. If the subject is only being presented "evidence" to balance the picture presented by the church, as is claimed, an open forum should be conducted with an opportunity for rebuttal from the opposing sides. Such is not the case, and the subject is at all costs kept away from any contact with church officials. The subject may say he does not wish such contact, but it should be noted that this is always said after the deprogramming session, which ends only when he or she breaks and not before.

Rehabilitation "fixes" the deprogramming, those involved claim, so that their results return fewer to the cults. It is said, "Disease is attacked in the name of cure," but if we allow this kind of rhetoric to apply to religion, we are in dangerous water. Of course, opponents refuse to call this a religion and thus will not let it be protected by freedom-of-religion claims. That begs the question of whether we as a nation have an agreed-upon dogmatic formula for "religion" or of whether some wish we did in order that annoying competitors could be removed legally.

The interview with Sun Myung Moon, as agreed, ended the investigation, but I had been determined to see Tucson for myself before closing up the manuscript. Before I went it seemed to me—and it still does—that Tucson stands as a symbol for the anti-Moon forces. It brings the opponents' claims into focus, but the unfortunate thing we witness is that the deprogrammers adopt the very tactics they accuse the movement of using: seclusion, artificially created atmosphere, constant mental pressure, removal of support, and the presentation of one side of the argument only, with no chance for open debate. Of course, they claim to have the "true position," so that whatever they do in the name of truth is justified.

The battle for the mind is undoubtedly a subtle one, but the claim to decide in a perfectly neutral atmosphere is a dream. In America we have agreed on the route of an open forum. We trust an atmosphere of pluralism that involves no physical coercion. Has the Moon movement violated that condition of freedom? The issue is not easy to decide, but deprivation of freedom by deprogrammers, I should think, can never be justified in the name of freedom, and probably it will be self-defeating. The journey to Tucson solved no problems, but it made some issues clear. It also convinced me of the dangers of secrecy and clandestine activities and pointed to the moral demand we have to try to keep all parties involved open to one another.

Tucson. Interview with deprogrammer who is a former church member. February 1977.

"Team captains have instructed their members to lie. It is at least a very, very significant practice that has not been directly stopped by Moon himself. I have never, ever heard him say anything about honesty in fund raising directly to his members. He may say it to you because he wants you to get an impression that he is honest. But I don't think he will say that to his members, because I think what he really wants is for them to collect the most money they possibly can. . . .

"It is very probable there has been a great deal of deception used by them in conversations with you. . . .

"I decided there were a lot of great things I had learned from this movement and I continue to feel that. . . .

"I feel the theology is extremely questionable in a number of variables. And when I came to that conclusion I felt very sure that this man in fact was not the messiah, that his ideas were familiar, lacked originality, at least the originality you would expect from the messiah, and that, therefore, his pretense of being the messiah made this whole movement something that was a very serious idolatrist proposition. And shortly after I started working as a deprogrammer. . . .

"I think the same ideas that I was having when I was in the movement are still operative, only now they reversed my direction. I still am highly motivated, only now I see evil in a different place and I want to fight it."

The Search for Origins In Japan and Korea

Out of the East it's coming,
Burning, beaming bright.
And all of the children come running—
Lord! What a wonderful sight.

—from a Unification Church song

If you know the character of the Japanese, you might suspect my visit to Japan was highly organized. My son, Grant, had gone out ahead of me to help, and once I arrived we worked around the clock, Japanese style, to cover a great deal in a short time. Japan was Reverend Moon's first mission country outside Korea, followed by the United States. This was not by accident but by design to follow a divine program. Knowing something of the long hostility between Japan and Korea, I went to Japan to try to solve one question. Given the generations of bitter feelings, how could an ex-Presbyterian Korean religious leader succeed in Japan where all things Korean are still held in poor esteem and where Christianity has had a minimal reception? I posed this question to an international mission team working in Japan made up of members from all over the world.

One answer is that the Unification movement in Japan, as everywhere, began as a youth–college-age movement, and racial hostilities among the young are not so deep as they are with an older generation. Furthermore, several Japanese leaders pointed out to me the latent sense of sin and the feeling of guilt prevalent among Japanese youth over their

Left: Japanese publications. *Right:* Japanese Moonies welcome author to dinner with a song.

past conquest and subjugation of Korea. This burden opened the young of Japan to a Korean-Christian message in a way no other Western Christian movement has been able to do in that country. One Korean boy testified that he had found the only real acceptance he had known in Japan among the Unification family.

The feeling one gets for the church in Japan is that of immense vitality and financial success. Membership is in the neighborhood of 400,000. Without question they are sure they have a role to play in Japanese moral and political life, aimed primarily in opposition to the growing radical left. They publish a newspaper that strives for international reporting. Everywhere they burst with the kind of growth psychology that marks the Japanese economy. Since my time in Japan necessarily had to be short, my son had gone ahead of me and toured outside Tokyo. After I arrived, we confined ourselves to visiting all the Tokyo centers of activity on a dawn-to-midnight schedule. Clearly, the Japanese church has been the key to the financial growth and success of the worldwide Unification movement as well as the origin of the life-style. However, it is both ironic and instructive about life within the church that I actually had to catch up with many of the Japanese (and Korean) leaders in the United States. Their business ventures, plus church conferences, bring them here constantly, frequently without much warning. Also, many of those knowledgeable about the early days of the church in the East are now more or less permanent residents in America.

71

Tokyo. Discussion at Unification Church headquarters with Japanese leaders. September 1976.

"The thoughts of Reverend Moon had an appeal to the Japanese youth. The teachings had a spiritual quality, but at the same time they were logical and scientific."

"The first missionary to Japan was truly a man of spirit. He could really transmit God's love to the people. He was a devout Christian, and this reached the heart of many young people who were seeking for that kind of quality."

"What may be distinct about the Japanese people is their desirability to work together, organize together. This living together in centers for your whole life more or less started in Japan. The Japanese leaders have a mission to improve the family feeling, to be together as a group, working together on a project. The Japanese church life-style, living together in a center, was exported to other countries. It was quite easy for Japanese but not so for other countries, who rely more on individualism."

"What impressed me most about the church was that there were people from all parts of the world, and yet they not only could live together but were working together to build something much greater than I had ever experienced. And I thought: Whatever force can unite people from such different backgrounds must really be the truth. And I wanted to know more."

"The entire purpose of the organization is to call forth to Japan to grow into a democracy in its true sense. We want eventually to lead the people into God's love."

"I came across the principle of not just working for your own nation but the basic concept of living for others, for the sake and benefit of others. To devote your life completely for the sake of others. This inspired me to almost an amazing degree. In each nation there is a very deep character, and we have to discover the true character of each one."

"Reverend Moon's ideology is that academic work should be for the betterment of the country, of society. For that purpose we gather the professors who have the desire to do something, to better Japan and Asia."

"I am a Korean, born in Japan. There never was a moment in my life that I was happy that I was born Korean. I was never proud of it here in Japan. But when I came across the *Divine Principle*, I came across courage. I gained courage and hope in life. I also gained pride in the fact that I was Korean and I need no longer be ashamed. I should work harder to dissolve the national rift or gap between people."

Washington, D.C. Interview with early leader from Japan. November 1976.

"I never saw such a person, a person who wants to give new life to other people. That really impressed me. . . .

"I started collecting garbage and reselling it for money. I started selling my blood a few times a month. I established many churches in different districts. I will never forget about that time. . . .

"After I came to the U.S. I was with Reverend Moon almost day and night for four years. But still I do not know how deep Reverend Moon is. I cannot penetrate him fully yet, he is so deep. . . .

"I know everything about where the money goes to. It really makes me angry when people say that we are getting money from the Korean CIA. If we would get money from them we would not have to work so hard. We could relax. . . .

"So far I have done so many things, but I don't think about it like I have done it. God did it through me. . . .

"Reverend Moon is always ahead of us, he has many new ideas."

New York City. Interview with early Korean missionary to Japan. November 1976.

"His appearance really disappointed me. He did not give me any impression of a saint or something, or a leader. But I believed in the *Divine Principle* strongly, and because of that, I could accept Reverend Moon. . . .

"I didn't go to any Korean community [in Japan]. The Korean community had already heard about the Unification Church. They had already a bad impression of the church. It would hinder me in spreading the Principle. I went straight to the Japanese people. I was the first missionary, but the Japanese police caught me and I was in jail for six months as an illegal alien. . . .

"When I had a group of about ten students I could not hide any longer. I was so poor. But we had a very good spirit. And that spirit is the tradition of the Japanese Unification Church today."

Washington, D.C. Interview with early Japanese convert and present church leader. November 1976.

"In 1966 Reverend Moon first came to Japan. At that time I didn't think of Reverend Moon as the messiah, but I did feel that Reverend Moon is the man who will save the world. . . .

"No matter how small the place, no matter how narrow the road, the Japanese people will reach their target. In addition to that, Japan ruled over Korea for forty years and also we waged a war against the U.S., so that brought the Japanese internally to some kind of sin-consciousness to those countries, and to pay for that all, Japan can use material things to pay their indemnity. That is special to the mentality of the Unification Church in Japan. . . .

"We had to live ourselves and so we started the garbage collecting and flower selling and then later to more sophisticated things. . . .

"In Japan there is a saying that if you meet ten people coming this way, six of them are either Communists or Communist sympathizers. Our members are busy with those Communist groups mentally every day. It is spiritually a big burden. The more the Communist forces come down on us the more we can grow spiritually and in capability. In the last two years there has been a rapid growth. . . .

"In the early days of the movement there was a problem with parents whose children would join. But gradually, the parents tend to think that the only hope lies in the children, and they have to trust them in what they do. There is not much problem with the Christian churches, for there is not much of a Christian foundation in Japan. . . .

"To meet with all these problems financial power is needed. We cannot say that what we have now is enough. We cannot be satisfied with that. We need much more to face that challenge. The pattern in the U.S. is imported from Japan."

Korea, of course, was the most important experience and the one I had been waiting for. Here lay the origins of the movement shrouded in mystery and controversy. I had spent part of a sabbatical year in Japan and felt I knew something of that country, but I had never been to Korea and had only heard that I would find it different. As my son and I came into the Seoul airport we were aware of one difference: it is a heavily guarded military base. No pictures may be taken. Customs is a long procedure. We were throughly searched and frisked. Our copy of the morning Japanese newspaper was taken away. When we stepped out of the airport we knew we were in a country living under a state of military alert.

The country, of course, is economically poor but in the midst of rapid industrial development. On every hill one sees a church—an Asian New England. It is a place literally bursting with religions—a Los Angeles gone wild. Unification doctrine is by no means the latest mushrooming new religion. Pentecostal faith healing now has the center of the stage. The Unification Church has become established and somewhat staid, but it is obviously alive and vital—in spite of the continual announcements of its death by its opponents. Officials estimate the membership at 280,000. In other countries the church is a youth movement. In Korea, even more so than in Japan, it spans all generations. Attending Sunday service is like 11:00 A.M. worship in any Protestant mission church. Observing the Unification Church as it now is in Korea, one gets a preview of how it may develop in other countries as time matures its members.*

To understand the birth of a new religion, we must learn something of its country of origin and context. I cannot pose as an expert on Korea, but I do know that, of all my visits and interviews, the trip to Korea and the discussion there provided the greatest illumination. And I suspect few outside Korea know much about the religious character of the country. It is, as Billy Graham has noted, one of the few places in the East of widespread Christian conversion in modern times. But by their own admission, Koreans tend to

---

*In spring of 1977, newspapers carried stories of the arrest of Unification Church officials in Seoul. Church sources had spoken of an imminent crackdown every time I asked about their friendly relations with the Park government. If there were ever mutual cooperation between the Unification church and the South Korean state, it clearly has come to an end.

be divisive and contentious. New religions spring up quickly and split into divergent groups almost as soon as they are established. The Japanese have the Samurai tradition of loyalty and conformity, but, by contrast, Koreans are individualists.

Thus we have a religiously fertile and volatile country where new revelations are a daily occurrence. Koreans think of their country as containing "the Jerusalem of the East," and it is interesting to note the similarities in the situation: generations of outside dominance, persecution of religions, occupation by foreign powers, and an inability to control their own affairs in peace. If you stand on the tip of a peninsula that has been so many times overrun and been the battleground of foreign powers, you have an entirely different feeling about religion than if you stand in the safety of the cornfields of Iowa. Here you sense the history of persecution, occupation, and wars, which so often are the soil from which religion springs. When the body is suppressed, the religious spirit takes on a new importance.

Sun Myung Moon is no new phenomenon in Korea, as indeed he is not in America, that ground upon which every new religion seems to flourish. But it is also true that, because of the tendency to divisiveness, the rise of any new religion in Korea is met with a certain fear and defensiveness. If you lived there, you could understand why the call he issued was not to form another new church but to start a movement of the Holy Spirit to unite all Christians, indeed all religions. Experiencing directly the lack of charity between churches and the wasted energy that religions use up in competing with one another, the call to unite all religious men and women for a common cause is a powerfully appealing one. The Holy Spirit Association for the Unification of World Christianity is the movement's original name.

In Korea, in the religion's formative days, the early converts constantly found relief in a message that offered a way to heal the wounds between warring and hostile religions. But, of course, it is an irony we must explore further that at least the first result of the movement has been to introduce greater division and tension. It is expected that hostile reactions will come at first. The issue is whether, in the long run, the goal to heal the breach between peoples and unify religions can be accomplished. In any case, it is a powerful objective that draws intense loyalty from many.

In addition to some understanding of the peculiarities and fertility of the religious soil in Korea, it is particularly helpful to see the development of this religion in its parallels to, and as an alternative for, Communism. In its formation it offered a counterpart to Communist doctrine on almost every score.

1. The Unification Church is centralized in its authority in the transitional stage.

2. The church promises, however, that a heavenly kingdom is coming and is possible on this earth—a time when power and temporal authority will no longer rule the day.

3. The Kingdom will come to be through gaining a knowledge of spiritual forces, not material forces, although material control is essential to spiritual victory.

4. The privileged few, the inner core, have this true understanding revealed to them. This gives them the power that comes from possessing the truth, which they are now bound to share with others. (This leads to the oft-mentioned charge of deception, which Communism faces too; both argue that everyone cannot assimilate the truth at once but must be led to it gently.)

5. There is an esoteric (for the faithful) vs. an exoteric (for the unconverted) teaching, since the truth of the *Divine Principle* cannot be thrust on everyone. Those who have accepted it are in a superior position to understand how the world and men are ruled and what needs to be done.

6. The Unification Church contrasts with Marxism in being totally theistically centered, something the outsider usually misses at first. The main task is to become "one with God" as opposed to the Marxist goal of unity with the proletariat.

Of course, Americans and Europeans became aware of Reverend Moon when he was already successful and when

Left: Sun Myung Moon, high school portrait. *Right:* Church school class photograph, February 27, 1941. Sun Myung Moon is in the front row, third from the left.

the church had become the owner of sizable pieces of real estate. As nearly as I could determine from my tour in Korea, the story of humble origin, imprisonment, and suffering is substantially true. The earliest disciples who followed him through these years, his family, his college friends, all report the same facts about his early life. It is interesting that his two cousins to whom I talked knew nothing of the "Easter revelation experience." This does not mean it did not take place, but it does mean that for a while he kept his own counsel about his mission.

Moon was born in a rural town in North Korea on January 6 (lunar calendar), 1920. His family converted to Presbyterianism when Moon was 10, and thus he grew up in a Christian context. His family reported him as quiet, serious, and given to spending time alone. On Easter morning in 1936, when he was sixteen, Moon reports later in life, Jesus appeared to him and told him he was chosen to attempt the completion of Jesus' mission. For the next nine years he struggled with this burden. Through much prayer and research he discovered the Principle which was to become the core of the *Divine Principle.* Spiritual battles with the cosmic forces of evil were waged, much as hermits report themselves beseiged and the center of spiritual struggle when they are alone in the desert. In 1938 he went to study electrical engineering in Japan, but in 1946, at the end of World War II, he began his public religious mission.

If the spiritual battle was won at that time, the physical

Left: High school class photograph. Sun Myung Moon is in top row, fourth from right. *Right:* Moon and other students away from home often cooked their own meals. Moon is at far right.

world had yet to reflect what he had accomplished. He moved to Pyongyang, and in June, 1946, he began to preach in the town that calls itself the "Jerusalem of the East." Early disciples report that progress was slow and living conditions meager. The land was under Russian Communist occupation, and Reverend Moon was arrested because of the agitation his preaching caused. Ultimately he was sent to a labor camp in February, 1948. As Solzhenitsyn has taught us, conditions in such camps are stark, but Moon managed to survive. One of the two remaining earliest disciples reports on visiting him in prison. She walked the hundred miles necessary to do so and testifies to the bleakness of the prison condition.

After the U.N. intervention in the Korean War, Moon was liberated on October 14, 1950, by U.N. forces. He located two remaining disciples and fled south to Pusan, arriving in January of 1951. He began to preach the Principle there, and members who joined the movement at that time tell of the struggle to survive in a crowded refugee town. Each follower worked to support himself, Reverend Moon as a laborer on the docks. They lived together under primitive conditions in a shack they built themselves, and they report the day Moon first announced having completed the writing of the draft of the *Divine Principle*. The public ministry begun in 1954 spread to Japan with its first missionary in 1958. Because of the traditionally bitter feelings between Japan and Korea, such a mission had to be

Top left: Three early disciples from the Pyongya\
days in 1956: Se Hyun Ok (left), Seung Do C\
(right), and Won Pil Kim (seated). According\
Unification sources, Kim helped Moon save\
former fellow prisoner with a broken leg when th\
fled south from Pyongyang. Together they push\
and pulled the man on a bicycle the six hundr\
miles to Pusan. *Top right:* The Pusan hut built fro\
U.S. Army ration boxes and mud in the summer\
1951. *Left:* Sun Myung Moon was liberated from\
North Korean labor camp by United Nations forc\
on October 14, 1950. Here, he is released from\
South Korean prison in 1955. He was held for thre\
months awaiting trial before the charges we\
dropped.

secretive, and the amazing thing is that it succeeded at all. In 1959, the first missionary came to America, and the movement now has mission teams in 120 countries. Moon married for the second time in 1960 and began his promised family. There are unconfirmed reports of other marriages, but at least it is clear that his first wife could not accept the religious role thrust on her. She opposed Moon for a time before that marriage was dissolved.

That is the simple story. Detractors treat it as a sham. Disciples view it as a life of torture, struggle, sacrifice, and eventual spiritual victory, surrounded by signs and portents of things to come. The interesting thing is that the same man can serve as the focus for both sets of feelings. We seem to need to find both hope and great ideals and to personify them in an individual. We also are frustrated and must find scapegoats to explain away our own failings, and we personify these outside ourselves. It would be easier if different figures each attracted a different focus. It is both intriguing and baffling when the same figure attracts hate and love.

Top: The first Unification Church, Seoul, 1954. Moon moved to Seoul in 1953. In 1954 he officially established The Holy Spirit Association for the Unification of World Christianity. *Center:* Church members gather outside early Seoul church, 1954. *Left:* Sun Myung Moon and Sang Ik Choi, first missionary. His success in Japan launched the Unification Church beyond the shores of Korea. *Right:* In 1959.

Opposite page, top three photos: Outings and picnics were one of the chief social functions of the impoverished early church. Moon's gaunt face reflects the stark prison years in these 1950s photographs. *Below:* Moon preaches on the providential significance of marriage the day before his wedding, 1960.

This page, top: An emotional prayer during an early church service, 1954. *Left:* Moon weds Hak Ja Han. Wedding portrait, 1960, traditional Korean wedding costume. *Right:* Mr. and Mrs. Moon, 1963.

Fortunately, we are dealing with a religious movement whose earliest converts are still alive. It is now possible to experience all these sources firsthand, but soon that will no longer be true. The earliest disciple still living is Mrs. Se Hyun Ok, now a venerable lady in her eighties. I spent an evening hearing her story of how she first met Moon at the beginning of his mission in the North, followed him through his prison days—regularly making the walking trip across Korea to take him food in the concentration camp—and then traveled South with him after the prisoners were liberated. I talked with the early disciples from the Pusan mud-hut days. They lived in close contact with Reverend Moon while he put his Principles down in written form. And these same early followers heard his doctrine preached orally before it ever took fixed form.

PHOTO BY AUTHOR

Left: Mrs. Se Hyun Ok. *Right:* Hyo Jin, the first son, on the occasion of his first birthday, 1962.

Seoul, Korea. Dinner conversation with Mrs. Se Hyun Ok, Moon's earliest disciple from the North. September 1976.

"During the period Reverend Moon taught families in North Korea, he told the families the *Divine Principle,* not just like a lecture, but in the preaching in the Sunday service or on Wednesday or Sunday nights. . . . The writing of the *Divine Principle,* the structuring of it, started in Pusan. . . .

"At that time in North Korea, all the members came to

Reverend Moon. He did not seek them out. They came to him. They were seeking revelation from God. I received a revelation about the coming of the messiah. God said that very soon the messiah would come. . . .

"One family would take care of Reverend Moon. He lived there. But all the members lived separately. On Sunday they would come together for worship. . . .

"Before Reverend Moon went to prison he had twenty followers. Then he was arrested by the police and went to prison. The followers lost confidence in him and they scattered. . . .

"When I first saw him in Pusan, he looked very dirty, in national Korean dress, very humble and dirty. The first impression was of a poor factory worker."

Seoul, Korea. Conversation with Moon's early followers. September 1976.

"I always expected the return of the messiah some day, but I never thought it would be in Korea. In his teaching he talked about the return of the messiah. We were in a small room, so I could see: His eyes were so bright. There was something different."

"Reverend Moon insisted, so I had dinner with his church family. It was all very humble, some rice and bean curd."

"The prayer of Reverend Moon was absolutely different. He was giving something to God, always giving."

"One day I went there and I asked him 'Why do you live here so humble like a beggar?' I said to him, 'How can I find out if these things are true or not?' and he said, 'You pray and you will find out if the teachings of Reverend Moon are true or not.'"

"When I first met him he was so skinny and very dirty and black."

"Reverend Moon told me that day was a very significant day, but I didn't know why. Later I learned that in that day he finished writing the *Divine Principle* for the first time [May 10, 1952]."

"The Christianity in Korea is really different from Western Christianity. Spiritually it is much higher."

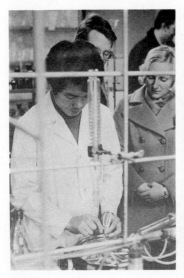

Left: A laboratory worker at the ginseng tea factory. *Right:* A Moonie working in a church-owned machine factory in Korea.

"It is general in Korea that Christians pray so much and cry."

"The pattern of services was rather different in this time. There were no schedules. People were just singing and praying. Everybody had a spiritual experience. It was a different style. They were always crying and shouting."

As a matter of routine we were taken to visit the titanium plant and the ginseng tea factory, both church enterprises. Central to the church's theology is its anti-Communist school lecture series, and I spent one morning receiving lectures on "victory over Communism." When we visited their largest training center, thousands were assembled to hear the tape of Reverend Moon's Washington Monument speech. Since I had just come from Washington, I found myself treated as a minor celebrity, as a witness who could report on that momentous event. Chairs are not used so that a great many more people can be accommodated in a room. Thousands were jammed together to hear the speech. They asked me to speak to the group and say a few words about the experience of watching the Washington rally.

Korea. Conversation with converts at training center outside Seoul. September 1976.

"Most members respond [to the question, Who is Sun Myung Moon?] first of all by saying that they can never forget what he has done for them."

"Some of these members have problems with their families when they join, and some of them had problems with the churches they came from. But here in Korea we have already passed that stage. It is much more easy now."

"The opposition of other churches is a great problem. But if we accept their opposition and if we love them as much as they oppose us, some day they will give up and surrender to our love, and then the problem will be solved."

"The teachings of Reverend Moon changed me. I feel now that we must live for others, for the well-being of others. Before joining the church I believed in living off other people. But the teachings of Reverend Moon changed me, and now I understand we must give ourselves for others."

"Before joining the church I was intoxicated often times and would smoke a lot. I was changed by the *Divine Principle* to a sacrificial life."

I spent one day interviewing people outside the church through contacts I had made before leaving America. These varied from impartial "old Korea hands" to bitter, fearful, and hostile opponents who talked darkly of reprisals. Wherever it has begun to be successful, the movement has aroused the same spectrum of emotions and active opposition. However, it was easy to detect the factionalism that characterizes most of Korean political and religious life. This contentiousness makes them a people at once capable of producing an intense religious response while at the same time splintering into factions which waste time and energy opposing one another. What is necessary to unite Korea, religiously and politically, in order to keep it from self-destruction? one keeps asking.

Seoul, Korea, Interview with a non–church member, a university teacher and early observer of the church. September 1976.

"I was looking for some place to really rely on spiritually. One characteristic is that all the intellectuals are there. They

Left: Christening of a church-owned fishing boat, early-1960s. *Right:* Reverend Moon enjoys *yut nori*, a Korean game, with church leaders in this late-1960s photograph.

are very rational; that kind of people follow him. . . . I had the impression that they didn't just believe like a machine, out of routine—they believed with some foundation, some basis. . . .

"At that time real bad rumors were going around about this Moon. . . .

"Always my attitude is this: not just to say that the Unification Church is wrong. They have something good and they have something bad."

Seoul, Korea. Interview with Protestant church mission leaders. September 1976.

"After the Korean War, there were many spirit religions developed in Korea. Part of it was a spiritual hunger after the terrible devastation."

"It has not died here, although it is not a powerful group in Korea, at least not that I am aware of."

"It has the Korean method of what we call syncretism. This has been the favorite religious method in Korea, take a little bit of something and something else and make your own thing."

"He is a modern version of what we used to call the Way of Heaven."

Seoul, Korea. Interview with Yonsei University official. September 1976.

"In various forms Koreans are quite taken by messianic hopes. . . . Particularly in the postwar period all sorts of sects have been sprouting up. . . .

"Moon burst into prominence essentially in the seventies. Up until 1965 he was just another of the various factioned sects growing up in Korea. . . . Korea was very ripe for religious movements of one sort or another. . . .

"The Christian church here is, as a whole, quite conservative, if not fundamental. . . .

"Korea is a country that for the past two hundred or three hundred years has been riddled by factionalism of all kinds, and factionalism has attacked the churches as everything else, so that almost any kind of dynamic leader very soon formed his own sect. . . .

"Why did the Christian church grow in Korea? In the end you have to say that the Holy Spirit moved."

I visited the lake where Moon goes to pray and meditate before major decisions. The cousins with whom he grew up met us there and told me anecdotes from his childhood as we sat under the arbor looking out at the lake. A friend from Moon's days as a university student described his demeanor in Japan, where they were all involved in underground Korean liberation and religious movements. From the beginning, Moon's religious doctrine had implications for political life, which is understandable given the Korean situation. I had a lengthy breakfast with the student-faculty group expelled from Yonsei and Ewha Universities in the days when the movement first began to explode with converts among the student generation. Unification doctrine is clearly syncretic. It grew out of the diverse and exploding religious milieu of its day, but it has consolidated its doctrine and its life-style into a tradition of its own.

Seoul, Korea. Breakfast meeting with teachers and students expelled from Christian universities May 11, 1955, for joining the Unification Church. September 1976.

"They forced us to select one of two things, the university or our religion."

89

"After the war their [students'] minds had a need for a strong belief. After not being able to go to church under the Communists, the Unification Church appeared to them as a very hopeful religion for the future."

"During the Korean War, the Communists would ask, Where is God? Can you believe that the heavenly kingdom will be established on earth? But Christians couldn't answer that. They couldn't solve the people's problem because they didn't have an answer. But the Unification Church can answer that."

"At the time many churches quarreled with each other. One pastor of a group began to hint against other groups. I wanted to believe, but there was no blessing in the churches, no grace."

"After the Korean War I was looking for something to overcome Communism. And in the Principle I found the answers I was looking for."

"Those who wanted to know the Bible and learn God's will couldn't get an answer from their pastors, because they were busy fighting each other. They couldn't get any satisfaction in their belief. At that time the Unification Church appeared."

"Everything was very confused, and Koreans didn't know which way to go. The Unification Church gave them real truth and showed them God's will, and they were very moved by that."

Now, of course, many of the early members of the Korean movement are spearheading the missionary effort in other lands. Some are part of Moon's close family of advisers, and they are particularly counted on to represent and to convey the early spirit of the movement to the new convert, who probably has never seen Korea and knows nothing of its heritage. The Korean and Japanese leaders obviously form the inner core and are the source of the movement's drive and vitality. One calls himself "the fighter" and took the name of David. Another is the military commander of spiritual growth. Another is quiet and thoughtful, one a spiritual seer. All are diverse personalities with pronounced individual perspectives. All, however, profess intense loyalty to the cause and to Moon's leadership.

Barrytown, N.Y. Interview with early member from Korea, now a church official. November 1976.

"I firmly believe in the Bible, I have no conflict with Christianity. . . .

"In Portland, Oregon, there was established on January 3, 1961, one of the first Unification churches in America. . . . We had four key people involved in the restoration of America up to 1972. On the West Coast, Mr. Kim and Mr. Choi, on the East Coast, Miss Young Kim and Colonel Pak. We are all different personalities. Miss Kim is the theologian; I am outgoing; Mr. Choi is the politician. . . .

"I am a fighter and I was fighting for him. . . . I trained the young people in every state. I was with the father so I carry authority; I have the fighting spirit. . . . I enjoy the kids. They know I am very harsh, but they accept it. They need discipline and direction. . . .

"Why do people listen? The spirit of God is behind him. God is using Reverend Moon; God's power is moving this movement. The problem is ordinary people look at the structure. This is a battle on God's side against Satan's side centered in man. This is a war. . . .

"But the problem is that there is jealousy. The spiritual father is Reverend Moon, and the physical parents are jealous. I don't think that this will stop. It will continue. . . . Any kind of new movement will have a repercussion from the family. We encourage members to write. We encourage respect for the parents."

Tarrytown, N.Y. Interview with early follower from Korea. November 1976.

"The Christian churches in Korea started to have internal struggles and separations among the different denominations. Because of these internal struggles I was very much disappointed. I almost lost my faith in the Christian churches. Then the thought came to me that I wanted to go to the mountains to pray to God and consult God how I could deal with this. . . .

"I was deeply concerned with the future of Christianity and also about the Second Coming. I knew about the existence of God and Satan, but I did not have actual, real experience with them. But after I went into the mountains I had that experience. That is the time I learned the tactic to deal with the attack from Satan. . . . I received a message from God not to wait for the messiah; not to expect him like a miracle, but to seek him among normal human beings. I was told that I was living in the last day, that God will send one group of people on this earth to lead other groups to fulfill his providence. That will be persecuted very much. Then I felt very strongly that this was the group God was talking about. Since that time I gave up my faith in the Presbyterian denomination and joined the group. . . . I found out that it is not the faith in the traditional religious thought that saved their lives, but in the new age the new truth only can save their lives. This was all in 1956. . . .

"To call one 'father' would be the most intimate relationship one could have with someone. It means you are closer to that person. Twenty years ago members didn't use that word as much as they do now. They call him father now because now Reverend Moon does not only give the strict word but he gives more love. He shows and expresses more love. Twenty years ago he was very strict. Just teaching. Because of that people used to call him master. Now many members call him father. Time has changed."

Tarrytown, N.Y. Interview with early church leader and interpreter from Korea. November 1976.

"These last four years were my golden age in a way, my most rewarding time. Reverend Moon and I practically lived together. And I had a chance to observe every aspect of Reverend Moon's life and learn from it.

"It is really an impossible task for me to interpret for Reverend Moon, because his message is so profound and sometimes abstract, based upon Oriental philosophies and an Oriental way of expression. He never uses a script. He will pray for hours and hours and uses inspiration. When we traveled, at two o'clock in the morning he would be on the floor praying. But he never writes. Until the last moment of speech he just prays. I have no idea what to expect. So the interpreter has no way to do the homework, except to pray also. . . . A good interpreter from the United Nations would never be able to interpret Reverend Moon, that is for sure. So I am not interpreting Reverend Moon by skill. It is not a matter of skill, it is not a knowledge of language that would do the job. It is a different kind of interpreting. I am interpreting Reverend Moon's spirit, his conviction. And my interpretation is by faith. I must be completely in line with him spiritually, become totally his instrument. I must be able to convey the soul, the spirit he is teaching to the people that are listening. If I am not fired up then it is no good, I cannot inspire anybody. . . .

"I could testify what kind of person he is, what kind of religious leader he is. I have no doubt in my mind that every time he spoke and every time I translated I was listening to the word of God. It was shouting out of my mind—this is the word of God, what a truth—that kind of inspiration and excitement. . . .

"Actually I am not a spiritual person per se, not one who has visions, hears voices. I don't have those kinds of experiences. I am a down-to-earth person. In his ministry he [Reverend Moon] never used abnormal supernatural power, or mystical. He is also a down-to-earth person. His weapon is only truth. He does not say mystic things. Never. His teaching is appealing to the human heart and inspiring the heart—to touch, move, and change it. . . .

"He says the worst enemy of you, blocking you from going to heaven, is your own self. Unless you destroy your own selfishness you will never be allowed in the kingdom of God. That has been the teaching of Jesus, of course. But through Reverend Moon this has become so clear to me. It made it real and put me in that action. In this respect I say I have spiritual growth. I am not near perfection. Yet I know I am trying each day to live up to that basic criterion that Reverend Moon established. . . .

"When I initially joined, [there were] about a hundred members in the Seoul area, and all over the country less than two or three hundred. Reverend Moon impressed me in two ways at the time. As a humble person living in a humble way. And the more impressive thing was that I had never seen a man work so hard. He was a completely self-disciplined man. He never slept more than two hours every day. . . . There is one thing that has never changed. His absolute belief or understanding and his conviction about God and the truth. At that time and now, it is just the same. He is like a rock, never tarnished or worn out, never changed. Reverend Moon never changes, never stumbles, never goes back and forth. His conviction on the worst day, in jail, or no matter what happened, is the same. He knows the eternal truth. He knows God. His teachings have an eternal quality. . . .

"In those days Reverend Moon would say that he would preach in America. And I thought, How could that be? And he said that he would have missions in 120 nations. And while he was saying that the Korean government was trying to smash the movement. He would insist. But at the time I

Over one million people jammed the Yoido Parade Grounds to hear Sun Myung Moon give the principal address at the World Rally for Korean Freedom, June 7, 1975.

thought, How could the movement grow worldwide? Impossible. Now twenty years later it is all happening, 100 percent. . . .

"Reverend Moon is bringing the world an alternative to Communist takeover. He is bringing an equally drastic change, even more so than Communism. But this is a God-centered way of life. Reverend Moon's goal now is Moscow. What he is saying is that Moscow is a symbol of Communism. We are destined to fight this and over-come Communism. Not in a military way, but in a religious way. Communism can only be overcome with a positive religious principle. . . .

"There is a master plan in the heart and mind of Reverend Moon. He has been in the ministry for over thirty years,

94

and in the first twenty years he never bothered with the materialistic thing. Never bothered. Only the spiritual. The last ten years he is engaging in business. . . . In restoration we must become a master of both—the spiritual and the physical world. He conquered the spiritual world, but now his goal is the kingdom of God on earth, that is early emphasized. . . . We need material things to build the Kingdom. We need the material wealth or power to teach and expand the truth. He is very realistic in that respect. He is a very keen business leader. From the Principle, our movement is now headed toward two parallel accomplishments. One is spiritual accomplishments, the teaching of the Principle, seminars, centers, et cetera. Also, we need a material foundation which will support the spiritual work and to build our living paradise. A real, literal kingdom of God on earth. . . .

"He wants to transfer the Japanese-given loyalty to a new direction [loyalty to the coming of Christ]. Right now in our movement the Japanese people have a major role everywhere because of their loyalty.

"People never thought any good could come out of Bethlehem—why Bethlehem? And the same way people are thinking now, Why Korea, that poor miserable country? . . .

UC/NFP

Sun Myung Moon prays at the Seoul training center, 1976.

"Reverend Moon sees as our pioneer job to set out a proper tradition. He emphasizes tradition, so that the tradition will live and succeed by the generation to come. Hard-working tradition, unselfish tradition. That is why Reverend Moon pushes other people to hard work. That suffering, pioneering experience will become a priceless gift for that person. . . .

"Our movement, our goal itself, is not a political one per se, to take over the government and run it. Reverend Moon clearly states that he wants to influence the leadership through a process of education. Reverend Moon is deeply committed to create leadership that can accept God and be superior over Communism. This is why he sometimes appears to be very political. He wants the Unification Church to grow so that it will become an influencing power. . . .

"I can sense some change. Now his teaching is more toward future leadership of our movement. He asks us constantly, What would you do if Reverend Moon dies? He is preparing now to give more freedom and flexibility to the matured leaders in our movement. . . .

"Do you know what the Unification Church's real strength is? People in the Unification Church are literally prepared to die for the cause. No army is stronger than the army which does not fear death. . . . That is the kind of army Jesus Christ had—his own disciples stoned to death, tortured. The Unification Church has already produced some martyrs here and there, but practically everyone is really ready to face martyrdom gloriously. Like in Yankee Stadium during the enormous storm. I felt the martyrdom. I really saw the strength of the Unification Church. Nobody took shelter. Nobody hesitated and wondered what to do. I have been in the Unification Church twenty years, but that was probably one of the most beautiful things I have ever witnessed. I reassured myself of the power and strength of the Unification Church. With that we cannot fail."

What Does the Doctrine Teach?

Reason has moons,
Yet other moons
Lie mirrored
In the sea,
Confounding our astronomers,
But, oh,
Delighting me!

—Lewis Carroll

Who's Afraid of Sun Myung Moon?

It is fascinating to see Sun Myung Moon receive intense devotion and love from his followers and at the same time draw derision bordering on hatred from those outside. In Korea, one even senses a fear, like one induced by the Mafia, among the opposition, and in this country the outspoken opponents speak of death threats. The mixture and the intensity of the emotion swirling around this man make one wonder if any calm, accurate appraisal is possible. His followers project more onto him than he claims. To them he is a symbol and focus of what is good. To outsiders he appears the perfect embodiment of the Antichrist. Who is this man? Should we fear or love him?

The first thing to say is that he makes no claim to be any more than a man. If Jesus was human, so are we all, although God calls some humans for a special office. Moon does claim to possess an unusual and a special spiritual receptivity, but, to all except the naturalist, the ability to communicate spiritually is not uncommon. There is also a

97

claim to suffering that is borne religiously and to the special appearance of Jesus to him announcing Moon's call to a mission. Yet, as one of Moon's Roman Catholic detractors said, "That's no problem for me. We've been having special visions in my church for centuries." There is no claim that the *Divine Principle* was revealed in whole cloth in some literal way but merely that the Principle of God's operation to restore humanity, which once was hidden, has now been made plain as the result of study and prayer.

Perhaps the most difficult question I asked the followers as I interviewed them around the world was, "What do you understand the role of Reverend Moon to be?" Contrary to what one might expect, their answers were far from uniform. They varied all the way from "a mirror in which I see myself truly" to "teacher" to "revealer" to "God's instrument" and "messiah" to the straightforward declaration that "he is the Lord of the Second Advent, the expected messiah returned." From all this it is clear that Moonies follow no consistent, prescribed public teaching on this matter and that each is allowed some latitude to make out his or her own opinions on the topic. Of course, all is not totally relaxed. Given the claims of the doctrine, one must determine Moon's role and the follower's relationship to it.

The other complication here is the members' calculated reticence about public declaration. Contrary to popular belief, when you travel in Moonie circles you are not constantly bombarded with claims about Sun Myung Moon. It is not standard procedure to blurt out on first meeting, "Moon is the messiah returned." Why not? Because the whole doctrine stresses the necessity for preparation, for indemnity to be paid, for study and struggle to precede any affirmation. This reticence is not perpetuated so much because only an inner core can know this truth and the outside world would not understand (although that is true) as because such conclusions are not easily reached and require extensive preparation.

The revealed Principle, the doctrine, is more central than the man, although the doctrine claims that the new expected age cannot come without a central figure. Does

Moon occupy that role, or will he occupy it? Remember one crucial point in asking this: Other divine missions have failed or come short of full realization. Since "God proposes, man disposes," we have no assurance that the messianic plan will succeed this time either. Fulfillment depends as much or more on the loyalty of followers than on the leader. Desertion thwarted Jesus, not lack of capacity or intent. Thus, we have no guarantee that anyone will fulfill the role, but we do live in an age of expectation and promise, one full of God's climactic effort. It is a time to try, and Moon is, according to Unification doctrine—at the very least—central to this attempt.

In making any conclusive appraisal, we are blocked by the ancient notion of the messianic secret. Those who know are enjoined not to say until the time is right. But the *Divine Principle* itself makes no personal claim for Moon, a fact many detractors overlook. In spite of this, is it an inner secret that the followers do share? This secretive element may be one reason the answers I received from followers are so undogmatic and variable. Unification members do feel the messiah is already on earth, that the time of God's attempt is ripe, and that the principle of divine action formerly hidden, which makes our understanding of scripture at long last certain, is now revealed. The Reverend Moon is calling the world to repent since the Kingdom is at hand.

"The Lord of Love has come to us . . . and we want to pass it on" run the lines of a song the Moonies sing. The feeling of received love is the main phenomenon detractors of Moon do not explain. Time and again the established members testify to the beneficial change that their study of the Principle and their association with Reverend Moon have brought to them. Given the sensational aspects of the movement, it is easy enough to fault him, but what then remains unexplained is the outpouring of self-sacrificing love, which so many report has changed their lives. The mood of the followers is one of selfless service for others, and that is hard to reconcile with the self-seeking motives the detractors attribute to Moon.

Are men and women "broken" by their association with

Moon? That, of course, is the heaviest charge and poses the most difficult question. If you take self-development and ego expansion as assumed personal goals, a person who becomes other-directed and God-centered will seem broken. The God-centeredness that is the core of Moon's teaching is missed by most outsiders. If the follower achieves this, he will be changed. Is that good or bad? What does it mean to save a person—to recreate him, to show a truthful way? Jesus came to embody an ideal of true love. Moon accepts and respects that goal of Jesus. Without commenting on whether he thinks he has come to embody the goal of love himself too, we can say that he is complicated and embroiled in battles because he feels the material world must be brought under control, too, before love can win the day.

At the banquet concluding the Fifth International Conference of the Unity of the Sciences in Washington, D.C., a gospel singing group sang for those assembled, including Reverend Moon, a song entitled "You've Got to Have a Pure Heart." This, of course, comes out of Unification doctrine. A "new line" must be established, or has already been established, which avoids the stain of original sin and offers humanity a fresh start. The issue is: Who has a pure heart? Most outsiders certainly do not see Sun Myung Moon in this role. In fact, his private motives are the most suspect. On the other hand, the symbol of the pure heart is what attracts the followers to the movement and inspires them to struggle to emulate Moon. But, even if a heart once becomes pure, can it be corrupted by the world around it? The Moonies think they can escape that traditional fate this time.

We should, then, be afraid of Sun Myung Moon. If he is a man with a pure heart bearing a message of love, the public at large has been rather unperceptive of this important fact. But then it always has been difficult to make the inner life visible to the outside world. If, on the other hand, he is corrupt, as the public press and much of organized religion seems to take for granted, destructive powers have come clothed in what many find to be very attractive garb. In

100

order to solve the puzzle of the man, we must fathom the deepest forces of love and hate residing in human nature and understand how they are called forth and focused on a target or a model. Just as we oversimplify ourselves, we oversimplify Sun Myung Moon, because it is so much easier to do that than to untangle the complexities of love and hate within us all.

What Does the *Divine Principle* Claim?

It is an interesting experience for a philosopher/theologian to deal with Unification thought. In the first place, if you do not agree with it, you have to be sure where you stand in contrast. I cannot give a full exposition of the *Divine Principle,* and it is questionable whether I am the one to try. I have already mentioned the esoteric quality of the doctrine, that it cannot simply be expounded without preparation. Yet, if we are to grasp the setting of the questions at issue, a brief statement is needed for those who have not studied the teachings of Sun Myung Moon. Few people, of course, know much beyond a handful of inflammatory statements. Most do not care to know more.

In attempting to explain the setting for the reader, I will not try to set down the detail of the doctrine. It is elaborate and does require study for any depth of understanding. But I will try to explain the main tenets of the movement as they become focal points for the thinking of the followers. In doing so, I will concentrate on the *Divine Principle,* in earlier times called simply the *Principle,* using its 1974 English translation. All doctrine and practice stem from these teachings, which were at first oral and then later elaborated and written down. The exact form these should have is still debated within the movement. These are new "scriptures," like the *Book of Mormon* and Mary Baker Eddy's *Science and Health.* More than the person of Moon, they form the core of the movement spiritually.

Before beginning an overview, I want to set down the brief theological statement drafted by a group of Unification seminarians. I discovered that the "meaningful day of

October 14," which they mention, is the day of Moon's liberation from the North Korean prison camp. Some of the declaration requires interpretation, I think, in order to be understood fully, but still it puts their belief in succinct form.

Declaration of Unification Theological Affirmations at Barrytown, New York October 14, 1976

We, the undersigned, proclaim the following twelve theological articles of affirmation on the meaningful day of October 14, 1976, to Heaven and Earth:
In order to promote the unity of
    (1) Christian theologies,
    (2) Christian denominations, and
    (3) Christian churches,
And
    (4) to accomplish an inter-faith movement that Heavenly Father has given us as a great commandment before the Glorious Day of the Lord of the Second Coming takes place, to build the Kingdom of Heaven on Earth for all mankind to live in peace and order and joy forever.

Amen.

Unification Theological Affirmations

1. *God.* There is one living, eternal, and true God, a Person beyond space and time, who possesses perfect intellect, emotion and will, whose deepest nature is heart and love, who combines both masculinity and femininity, who is the source of all truth, beauty, and goodness, and who is the creator and sustainer of man and the universe and of all things visible and invisible. Man and the universe reflect His personality, nature, and purpose.

2. *Man.* Man was made by God as a special creation, made in His image as His children, like Him in personality and nature, and created to respond to His love, to be the source of His joy, and to share His creativity.

3. *God's Desire for Man and Creation.* God's desire for man and creation is eternal and unchanging; God wants men and women to fulfill three things: first, each to grow to perfection so as to be one in heart, will, and action with God, having

their bodies and minds united together in perfect harmony centering on God's love; second, to be united by God as husband and wife and give birth to sinless children of God, thereby establishing a sinless family and ultimately a sinless world; and third, to become lords of the created world by establishing a loving dominion of reciprocal give-and-take with it. Because of man's sin, however, none of these happened. Therefore God's present desire is that the problem of sin be solved and that all these things be restored, thus bringing about the earthly and heavenly kingdom of God.

4. *Sin.* The first man and woman (Adam and Eve), before they had become perfected, were tempted by the archangel Lucifer into illicit and forbidden love. Through this, Adam and Eve willfully turned away from God's will and purpose for them, thus bringing themselves and the human race into spiritual death. As a result of this Fall, Satan usurped the position of mankind's true father so that thereafter all people are born in sin both physically and spiritually and have a sinful propensity. Human beings therefore tend to oppose God and His will, and live in ignorance of their true nature and parentage and of all that they have lost. God too, grieves for His lost children and lost world, and has had to struggle incessantly to restore them to Himself. Creation groans in travail, waiting to be united through the true children of God.

5. *Christology.* Fallen mankind can be restored to God only through Christ (the Messiah), who comes as a new Adam to become the new head of the human race (replacing the sinful parents), through whom mankind can be reborn into God's family. In order for God to send the Messiah, mankind must fulfill certain conditions which restore what was lost through the Fall.

6. *History.* Restoration takes place through the paying of indemnity for (making reparations for) sin. Human history is the record of God's and Man's efforts to make these reparations over time in order that conditions can be fulfilled so that God can send the Messiah, who comes to initiate the complete restoration process. When some effort at fulfilling some reparation condition fails, it must be repeated, usually by someone else after some intervening time-period; history therefore exhibits a cyclic pattern. History culminates in the coming of the Messiah, and at that time the old age ends and a new age begins.

7. *Resurrection.* The process of resurrection is the process of

restoration to spiritual life and spiritual maturity, ultimately uniting man with God; it is passing from spiritual death into spiritual life. This is accomplished in part by man's effort (through prayer, good deeds, etc.) with the help of the saints in the spiritual world, and completed by God's activity of bringing man to rebirth through Christ (the Messiah).

8. *Predestination.* God's will that all people be restored to Him is predestined absolutely, and He has elected all people to salvation, but He has also given man part of the responsibility (to be accomplished through man's free will) for the accomplishment of both His original will and His will for the accomplishment of restoration; that responsibility remains man's permanently. God has predestined and called certain persons and groups of people for certain responsibilities; if they fail, others must take up their roles and greater reparations must be made.

9. *Jesus.* Jesus of Nazareth came as the Christ, the Second Adam, the only begotten Son of God. He became one with God, speaking the words of God and doing the works of God, and revealing God to the people. The people, however, rejected and crucified him, thereby preventing his building the Kingdom of God on earth. Jesus, however, was victorious over Satan in his crucifixion and resurrection, and thus made possible spiritual salvation for those who are reborn through him and the Holy Spirit. The restoration of the Kingdom of God on earth awaits the Second Coming of Christ.

10. *The Bible.* The Old and New Testament Scriptures are the record of God's progressive revelation to mankind. The purpose of the Bible is to bring us to Christ, and to reveal God's heart. Truth is unique, eternal, and unchanging, so any new message from God will be in conformity with the Bible and will illuminate it more deeply. Yet, in these last days, new truth must come from God in order that mankind be able to accomplish what is, yet, undone.

11. *Complete Restoration.* A proper understanding of theology concentrates simultaneously on man's relationship with God (vertical) and on man's relationship with his fellowman (horizontal). Man's sin disrupted both these relationships, and all the problems of our world result from this. These problems will be solved through restoration of man to God through Christ, and also through such measures as initiating proper moral standards and practices, forming true families, uniting all peoples and races (such as Orient, Occident and Negro), resolving the tension between science and religion, righting economic, racial, political, and educational injus-

tices, and overcoming God-denying ideologies such as Communism.

12. *Second Coming or Eschatology.* The Second Coming of Christ will occur in our age, an age much like that of the First Advent. Christ will come as before, as a man in the flesh, and he will establish a family through marriage to his Bride, a woman in the flesh, and they will become the True Parents of all mankind. Through our accepting the True Parents (the Second Coming of Christ), obeying them and following them, our original sin will be eliminated and we will eventually become perfect. True families fulfilling God's ideal will be begun, and the Kingdom of God will be established both on earth and in heaven. That day is now at hand.

We affirm and proclaim before God and Man these theological articles as statements of our faith on this Fourteenth day of October in the Year of Our Lord, Nineteen Hundred Seventy Six.

[*Here follow the signatures of thirty-eight seminary students.*]

As we now turn to explore the *Divine Principle,** a word needs to be said about its formation and its status. Of course, this in itself is a subject for a long book and is not my specialty, although learning something about the formation of new scripture is fascinating business. The early disciples report that Moon's teachings to the first group were oral, not written, but that they did contain what is considered the core of the present *Divine Principle.* The same disciples testify to having been present when the wording of the first draft was finished in Pusan. According to accounts, aspects and elaborations and particularly historical supporting material, were added in later editions. The work grew and had assistance in reaching its present form.

Where did the doctrines come from prior to their formation in Sun Myung Moon's mind? Korea at the time was a boiling caldron of religious views and teachers, and

---

*Published by The Holy Spirit Association for the Unification of World Christianity. Washington, D.C., 1973. All page numbers in this section refer to this edition.

nowhere does Reverend Moon claim that each word somehow came to him as a direct revelation. Syncreticism, observers report, is a religious way of life in Korea. Yet the insights were granted to him. His name does not appear as author on the title page, because he literally does not take the ideas to be his own. What were his sources of inspiration? "Prayer and the Bible"—this reply was snapped back at me by one leader when I asked the question. That will not satisfy scholars, and undoubtedly there are many historical antecedents to the *Divine Principle* as there are to all important works. Still, it was not a bad answer for the curious.

The *Divine Principle* begins by assuming that there is a universal struggle to gain happiness (p. 1). There is an "original mind" in man, like an unfallen nature, which seeks good and hates evil, but there is a contradiction in man as we know him. Sin introduced this contradiction, and the problem is to restore man to his original undivided mind (p. 3). Religion and science must be united. Philosophers cannot end human misery, and Christianity has turned into a "dead body," unable to fulfill man's need (p. 6). However, we cannot have spiritual happiness apart from true physical happiness (p. 8), so the Principle aims at a dual restoration, one which brings the physical realm into harmony with God as much as the spiritual. It must work on two fronts simultaneously, trying to unite them both to God's original purpose.

In order for this dual transformation to occur, "a new expression of truth must appear" (p. 9), since existing doctrines have proved inadequate. The issue involved in this assertion is whether God's revelation is closed or still open. As ought to be obvious, the Moonies are not biblical literalists; nor are our present scriptures wholly adequate for them. The vision of God has faded, they believe, so that the mission of the new truth is to enable us to "know God as a reality" (p. 10). However, the key to this new dispensation is the ideological confrontation of democracy and Communism (p. 11). Just as material and spiritual are linked, there is a political duality in the doctrine. Truth should unite all existing religions, but the doctrine clearly sides with the victory of theism, represented by democracy, over atheism, represented by Communism.

The aim is for all men to live in brotherly love under God as our parent (p. 12), but the means to achieve this pit one ideology against another. The new world, however, is coming in our own time. This is the power of their call. The sinful history of man, dominant until now, will be liquidated—an amazing promise. "Restoration" is the aim and is their key term. It is the counterpart of resurrection in traditional theology. God has a master plan he works out in orderly fashion. The *Divine Principle* is, in brief, the disclosure of that plan and thus a key that unlocks the misunderstood aspects of Scripture.

The new truth has appeared, and Sun Myung Moon is God's messenger—that much of the claim about Reverend Moon is quite clear. In his early life he lived through trials and fought satanic forces and through this brought to light heavenly secrets by communion with God (p. 16). No one has fully known the original plan for the creation of man and the universe. Parts were known, but God's plan in its clarity has been revealed only in our time, according to God's providential operations (p. 19). God has dual characteristics, as all things do, and it is crucial for us to understand this intended duality in all creation. Positive and negative characteristics (not a dualism of good and evil) are present in God, for example, male and female aspects (p. 24). Nature operates on a "give-and-take" principle, and so do man and God.

An elaborate metaphysics accompanies these doctrines, but I shall omit reporting that, partly for simplicity of statement and partly because there is some evidence that the metaphysical and historical framework was worked out later than the core of the Principle. *Give-and-take action* is a key phrase in all discussion, as is *horizontal* and *vertical power,* and much natural and human process is analyzed with these terms (p. 28). *Subject* and *object position* are also key interpretive concepts, and the self is designed to be God's object. *The Fall* means that man was cut off from a give-and-take relationship with God, and to restore that is our first goal (p. 30). This can be done by uniting with Jesus in a perfect give-and-take relationship—a doctrine not far from traditional Christianity except it is put in different concepts.

Four-position foundation is another important and interpretive concept, the primary example of which is God, husband and wife and their offspring (p. 30). This explains part of their emphasis on *family*, since a God-centered family is the only way to restore this four-position foundation. No individual can do it alone. Thus, individualism in religious life is self-defeating. The doctrine is communal, with God and family foremost. The body and mind must unite, and together center on God. The goal, then, is for a perfected man and woman to become husband and wife and, centering on God, form a perfect family. Together they become the center of all creation. Centering on God, they can establish the kingdom of God on earth (p. 36). God created this center, but it was lost when Adam fell. Now the time has come to restore it (p. 39).

The purpose of man's existence is to return joy to God, a refrain that appears in many of our traditional catechisms (p. 41). However, the anthropomorphism of God in the Principle is clear. "God's joy is produced in the same manner as man's" (p. 42). Thus, to say that man can "attain deity" is not so startling a statement (p. 43) when we realize how human God's joy is. God and man were intended to be close in nature, not radically divergent. *True Parents* are those who have been washed of the original sin of the Fall, the separation from God, and now live centered on God. The notion of True Parents is central to Unification life and thought, but it is not popularly understood. It means the establishment of a new lineage today, centered again on God and producing joy. Publicly, the notion draws violent reaction from parents who feel it rejects natural family bonds. The church does not intend this but merely wants to say that the bond with God is higher.

Love is central to God's nature, but Adam and Eve did not establish a God-centered family, and all men and

108

women have suffered from that rupture. As is easily seen, Old Testament themes form the core of the doctrine, rather than concepts beginning with Jesus. God, however, also operates "mathematically." He governs his relationship to man and the world according to sets of significant numbers, for example, three, twelve, the 120 countries into which their missionaries have been sent, as well as the numbers and times of the elaborately staged mass weddings or blessings. Central to Unification doctrine of man is the notion that we cannot reach perfection until we have acquired the ability to rule the rest of nature. Spiritual growth is not enough; all advance must be simultaneously physical. Their stress is thus on industrial development and the conscious striving for political and material muscle. Man is the center of harmony and can provide the mediation between the spiritual and physical worlds (p. 59). However, he does not seek power for his own purpose, but in order to bend it to God's purpose.

Jesus came as such a perfected man in flesh and in spirit (p. 60), but the realization of the kingdom of God in heaven must await the realization of the kingdom of God on earth. As you can see, this is not a doctrine that abandons the physical for the spiritual but rather asserts that the kingdom of God on earth comes first (p. 62). In this plan, man has control of his destiny, but within limits of the spiritual forces at play around us, of course (p. 63). Because man fell, however, Christ must come again to inaugurate the earthly role first (p. 69). Eve and Satan had an illicit sexual relationship, which gives a Freudian reading to the cause of man's fall (p. 80), but this new version of original sin does explain the church's puritanical prohibition of premarital sex and the downplaying of the role of sex for enjoyment even in marriage.

Man was created to live in accordance with the Principle, but illicit love made him deviate (p. 82). Thus, only love has the power to restore us to follow God's principle, but it must be a love centered on God and not on human desire—hence, their system of arranged marriages. Adam and Eve were immature and could not establish a relation-

109

ship of love centered on God and so they fell (p. 84). Now it is our job to mature love and accomplish the aim where they failed. We need to establish a world in which Satan can never act; but God cannot restore us by force. God in this respect is bound (p. 85), but men can accomplish restoration if they follow the proper guidance, which now has been given. The world of evil can be turned around by man and centered on Christ to realize the kingdom of God on earth (p. 86). The call to march is sounded.

In an interesting parallel to American "social gospel," the Principle proclaims the time has come when man has received the power to change the world toward God's purpose. True Parents can uncover the root of sin and liquidate it (p. 89). That is the religious function of True Parents as opposed to biological parents. *Freedom* means following the way of the Principle, and all other freedom is simply license, since God-centeredness alone restores man to his intended powers. Otherwise, as Saint Paul agrees, you are simply in bondage to sin. We fell at first because nonprincipled love became stronger than the directive power of God, so this must be reversed (p. 93). It is now up to us: Humanity can "restore the original nature of creation by the power of principled love" (p. 94)—quite a challenge.

God did not intervene to prevent the Fall, since he works only within the Principle and does not restrain man's freedom outside that. The purpose of human life is to return joy to God, but to do this people must know God's will and live according to it (p. 100). A person can become one body in unity with God, and this merging of divine and human self is the Principle's goal. A person of perfected individuality can never fall once he or she has reached that level, which Adam and Eve did not. God intended us for the kingdom of heaven on earth and not for a future existence in some heavenly sphere alone (p. 100). A new day has dawned. As evidence of it the church points to the formation of a worldwide cultural sphere. The new blend will include all forms of religion but center on Christianity (p. 107).

The Last Days are here, but this means that an age of hell on earth will be transformed into a kingdom of heaven on earth (p. 112). Jesus came to restore this ideal world, but he could not complete the task. This was not a result of failure on his part but of the disbelief of a faithless generation. Consequently, the completion of God's will was postponed until the time of the Lord's Second Advent. Jesus was pure, as all orthodox theologies assert, but the people's failure made it possible for him to accomplish only a spiritual salvation (p. 113). "My kingdom is not of this world." Few disagree that the physical order has not changed markedly since Jesus' time, and the traditional belief in the necessity of his Second Coming supports this. "Christ will come again" (p. 116). Today we are in the Last Days, finally.

We are entering a new age. The spiritual standard of fallen man is being restored (p. 120). God restores heavenly sovereignty by degrees (p. 124). Neither Noah nor Jesus destroyed the sovereignty of evil completely, but today man has restored his spiritual light (p. 128). Biblical words express the truth, but they are not full truth. (Unification doctrine is far from a biblical literalism.) There must be a scientific expression of truth (p. 131). A new truth must elucidate the Bible so clearly that all people can recognize and agree with it. "Jesus died on the cross without being able to say all that he wanted to say because of the disbelief of the people" (p. 132). The words Jesus left unuttered are not to remain secret but are to be revealed in the Last Days. The *Divine Principle* is, then, "secret sayings" now being uttered publicly.

Our task is to find the central figure of the new history, but his coming is apt to be rejected by Christians now just as it was by God's chosen before. However, spiritual things can be perceived by prayer, which makes intense prayer central to restoration. There is a Completed Testament Age as well as a New Testament Age. A man without original sin can multiply children of goodness who then "are not in need of a savior for the redemption of their sins" (p. 141). The Cross of Jesus left man's original nature unrestored, which process must now take place. "Jesus did not come to die on the cross" (p. 143) but to restore the whole earth.

Jesus' crucifixion was the result of the ignorance and

111

disbelief of the people and was not God's predestined plan (p. 145). This is a God who has definite intentions but who also gives very considerable freedom to mankind to execute those intentions. Jesus' crucifixion prevented the fulfillment of physical redemption, and Christ must come again. Jesus established the foundation of spiritual salvation but left physical salvation for the time of the Second Advent (p. 150), actually a rather traditional notion. The failure of John the Baptist to support him caused Jesus to take the way of crucifixion, but until the present no one has been able to reveal this "heavenly secret" (p. 163). We have lived through the two-thousand-year period called the "providential age of prolongation" (p. 174).

We are now in an age when men can communicate directly with God and with the spiritual world again, as we did before the Fall (p. 177). Those who are first to believe in the Lord of the Second Advent will cooperate with him in setting up the conditions of indemnity for restoration on a worldwide basis (p. 180). The total number of saints needed by the Lord of the Second Advent is the book of Revelation number of 144,000 (p. 180). Spirit men and earthly men will cooperate. The central person must set up the condition of indemnity corresponding to the debt of sin (p. 186), and this must pass from the individual to the family to the nation and to the world. All spirit men and women in Paradise will descend to become earthly saints and cooperate with us in the Last Days.

The Fall of Man was not God's predestination but man's free responsibility (p. 194). Thus, "God's purpose of creation can be fulfilled only by man's accomplishment of his portion of responsibility" (p. 197). In this sense, salvation is man-dependent, and the central figure in charge of the mission is also crucial. Technically speaking, God has 95 percent responsibility, man 5 percent, but that 5 percent is the key to accomplishment just as much as God's will or power (p. 198). The "central figure" in charge of the providence of restoration must be born out of a chosen nation (p. 200). Jesus is not God, except as any perfected person is one body with God (p. 209). As the traditional affirmation goes, Jesus was a man no different from us, except for the fact that he was without sin (p. 212).

There are Cain-like and Abel-like figures, but now the Cain-like should obey and surrender to the Abel-like (p. 246). Noah and Abraham were central figures in the restoration drama of their time, but their missions never came to completion. God's power cannot alone fulfill the providence of restoration; in that respect he is limited. Restoration can only be fulfilled by man's joint action with God (p. 238). The secret meaning of the words of the Bible are not knowable without understanding the principle of God's providence. This is what "Divine Principle" means (p. 285). God cannot grant grace unconditionally (p. 341). The Lord of the Second Advent must be born on earth, in flesh, as Jesus was (p. 369). He must restore the foundation to receive the messiah, starting on the family level and broadening to national and world levels (p. 369).

An elaborate historical and mathematical analysis of persons and ages is connected with this dramatic outline, but these exemplify the doctrine rather than extend it. Christian democracy creates the right environment to receive the messiah properly, while the satanic world is headed toward a Communistic society. There must come a political society and an economic foundation centering on God's ideal. In these beliefs Unification thought is millennial and theocratic, but these concepts must be understood in their special senses. World wars tend to be the inevitable way to set up the worldwide conditions for indemnity, but, of course, wars will disappear in the Completed Testament age (p. 477).

There is to be a uniting of all religions. Christianity, however, is not simply one among many but was set up as the central religion, with the mission to fulfill the purpose of all religions (p. 480). There is a prediction of the inevitability of a Third World War (p. 491), but in some instances this has been softened to a spiritual battle, not necessarily a shooting war. But there will be a final confrontation to bring perpetual peace (p. 493). God, believers are convinced, will let his prophets know all the secrets concerning the Second Advent before actualizing it—which implies an assumption about God's openness of procedure that I personally doubt. The period for the Second Advent began right after the First World War. Christ must come again to complete physical salvation, but the nation of the East where Christ will come again is none other than Korea (p. 520). The Korean people will become the Third Israel.

History is portrayed as the restoration of mankind to God, and all historical developments must be seen in light of this providential significance. Central to this process of restoration or salvation is the advent of the messiah, who is to establish the kingdom of God on earth. In order for the messiah to come, people must fulfill certain conditions, according to the principle of restoration through indemnity. A central figure must appear to do certain deeds (such as Noah building the Ark) in order to make a Foundation of Faith. This symbolically indemnifies Adam's failure to follow the will of God. It also separates humanity from the satanic world so that God can claim it.

Next, a Foundation of Substance must be set whereby a symbolic condition for the removal of man's fallen nature is made. The archangel should have obeyed Adam and not have misled him. This failure must be restored. Abel was chosen by God, and Cain should have escaped the dominion of Satan by giving up his privileged position as elder brother to receive God's blessing through Abel. By a Cain-like person's following an Abel-like person and receiving God's blessing and guidance through him, a symbolic condition for the removal of our fallen nature is made. On this basis, God has a foundation upon which he can send the messiah. Man then must receive the messiah and cleanse the original sin. All of history moves toward that purpose. From the time of Adam until the time of Jesus, God had been trying to send the messiah.

When certain central figures fail to fulfill this mission, God's will to send the messiah cannot be realized. Thus, there have been cycles of preparation repeated at various times in history, although history is seen as having a linear time element as well. Preparation occurs not only on the specific, individual basis but on economic, political, national, and global levels as well. The importance of a Foundation of Faith to a Moon follower is seen in any physical accomplishment, such as the Yankee Stadium rally, fasting, or the renovating of a building. All such activity is a condition. The Foundation of Substance is found in witnessing, whereby a member whom God can trust will prepare a potential follower to receive the words of God as a preparation to actually receiving the messiah. The Abel figure must gain the trust of the Cain figure who can then receive God's love and truth through the Abel figure.

Messianic expectation is deeply rooted in the Korean soil, which gives Koreans a certain affinity with the Jews. To suffer occupation and persecution has always bred such hopes and given deep spiritual roots to religion. But the above account is a brief exposition of the doctrine and is not meant as a critical evaluation. The questions it raises must wait, but the doctrine does touch every crucial point about which Christians must decide, beginning with a specific view of the nature of God and his mode of operations. Jesus prayed, "thy kingdom come," and the issue is whether and how God intends to answer Jesus' prayer. When the followers say, "God has given us truth," they mean the Principle. And since they equate power and truth, they expect to succeed.

The Old Testament gave Christians the story of spiritual struggle and preparation which prepared them for a later message, but it is one that we often lose with the birth of a New Testament "softness." Unification doctrine clearly puts us back into a time of spiritual struggle. Has the "completed Testament" brought us back to the Old Testament again, so that we are waiting for the messiah once more? The way to do this, they tell us, is not to discard existing Christianity but to unite all Christians in a mood of expectancy.

What Does the Master Say?

Sunlight beaming forth in the East, from the Fatherland,
Bringing tidings of a new world to families in the field.

—from a Unification Church song

Part of the sensational exposé material circulated by opponents of the movement contain quotations selected from the supposedly secret sayings of Reverend Moon. These turn out to be excerpts from *Master Speaks,* a collection of the recorded and transcribed talks that Moon makes to gatherings of the church. These have an in-house quality about them, and church doctrine does indicate that those outside cannot be expected to understand in the same way a follower who has studied can. We also need to know the situation of the talk and the particular people being addressed, members assert. But the "esoteric" quality is not quite so startling after one has read one or two hundred transcripts. You realize that, like unrefined scripture before our biblical documents were sorted out, you are dealing with material that can be quoted to prove a variety of things.

To the insider, these words are deeply spiritual and the soruce of profound personal guidance. To the antagonist, Moon's sayings seem like weird utterings of an egomaniac with a slightly sinister quality. For instance, on the street outside Moon gatherings you are handed anti-Moon propaganda with lists of selected quotations that are inflammatory on impact. On the other hand, one national church leader volunteered to me his own collection of favorite quotations taken from the same material, and these cast Moon in the role of a spiritual guide. The interesting thing is that both are true. Checking the sources, you find that both those who select to discredit and those who select to support can find their base in the texts.

To illustrate the contrast here, first, are quotations often used in anti-Moon literature:

The whole world is in my hand, and I will conquer and subjugate the world. If the U.S. continues its corruption,

116

and we find among the senators and congressmen no one really usable for our purposes; we can make senators and congressmen out of our own members.

Upon my command to the Europeans and others throughout the world to come live in the U.S., wouldn't they obey me?

Master needs many good-looking girls—three hundred.

We can embrace the religious world in one arm and the political world in the other. With this great ideology, if you are not confident to do this, you had better die. Are you resolved for that, and confident for that? (Yes!)

If our foundation has been laid, are we going to be confident persons or not? (Yes!) Then we will win the battle. This is our dream, our project—but shut your mouth tight, have hope and go on to realize it.

My dream is to organize a Christian political party including the Protestant denominations, Catholics, and all the religious sects.

And even on earth, whoever goes against you, that man must be subjugated, and he *will* be subjugated.

Mobile team activities are like guerilla warfare; hitting one place, moving to another, attacking another, and moving on. We don't have any home base; from one day to another we are moving.

The time will come, without my seeking it, that my words will almost serve as law. If I ask a certain thing, it will be done. If I don't want something, it will not be done.

Much of the meaning of the above quotations can be explained when one consults the text of the talk and reads it in the context of what is being said. However, my point is not to indicate how one might interpret these quotations or to question how they could be understood by one who reads them with no further background. I want, rather, to give the reader some idea of the scope and variety of these speeches and sayings, so that he or she gets some feeling for the range of the material we are dealing with.

Against the above, consider this selected list of Moon sayings offered me by one church leader:

117

We need to be so broadminded as to save even Satan. We need to be broadminded enough to draw the whole of the world to our side.

We must be connected to God or we cannot last to eternity. Before being able to realize the ideal world you must realize the presence of God working in you.

Love people like they were your own brothers, sisters, or your children. Children must love their parents like they love God.

We would construct a new society through love. A heavenly kingdom of heart. Do not let resentment grow in your heart.

If you make mistakes in loving each other you destroy yourselves and your descendents. . . . Love is the most dangerous—most precious. . . . Love must come from the Divine Center, through the central point.

Divine Love does not invade. It melts people. Divine Love must dominate the whole world.

Look at your parents. They brought you the gift of life to enter the kingdom of Heaven. Respect parents like they were God. We must praise older people.

When you hear Sun Myung Moon speak in this way, you can hardly imagine it is the same man quoted earlier. We are, of course, dealing with the phenomenon that most religious literature is wide-ranging, often lacks consistency, and defies reduction to a single line, modern interpretive techniques notwithstanding. The interesting thing is that the followers tend to use a spiritual reading while the detractors use quotations that make you wonder how any sane person could either offer or follow such advice.

To the above two contrasting sets of quotations, let me add selected passages from my own reading of *Master Speaks*. I will indicate only dates of the speeches rather than titles.

"Our movement is not to sacrifice the individual, family, tribe, or nation for the benefit of the Unification Church, but to sacrifice ourselves for the benefit of the whole nation and for other churches."
—December 11, 1971

"If there was a good environment prepared for him, with all the people around him administering to him [Jesus], something different from what we have in the biblical record could have happened. In order for him [Jesus] to be able to establish the kingdom of God on earth, he must have been able to establish the Kingdom right in his own family first. . . .

"To be reborn, man must have True Parents. When the Lord comes, first he must find a bride and then he must form a God-centered family. If True Father and True Mother become one and love each other, then God would come down and become one with them on earth. That is the will of God's restoration. . . .

"Therefore, when the Lord comes again, there must be disciples and a religious group like Judaism, which welcomes and prepares the bride for the Lord. There must come out a new organization which will prepare all these things; that is the Unified Family.

"The reason why the year 1960 became the turning point of history was because the foundation of new True Parents was laid down then."

—December 26, 1971

"Do you think God's Will will be realized by following Western style? It cannot be done. From now, we have to make new customs, new tradition, new culture, new life, a new way of living, new morality, new laws. Are you ready? . . .

"With the whole of the spirit world mobilized like that fighting against the evil spirits, then the restoration of the world will come about in the nearest possible future."

—December 29, 1971

"When you begin to be loved by God, and to know God's love, that is the starting point of human love."

—January 2, 1972

"Before he [Master] started his work on earth he worked in the spirit world. He fought and won the victory there. Because of such conditions, he could establish a victorious kingdom on earth. In the seven years after 1975 we have to break through. . . .

"You have to become one with Master, and link the many traditions. He does not like the separate groups. Some talk of Mr. Kim's group or Miss Kim's group, or Mr. Choi's group. He does not like that."

—January 3, 1972

119

"Your witnessing technique is the most important thing. Always think, How can I attract this person to me? There is only one method for doing this. That is the spirit of serving that person. When you are going to do something to take advantage of the person, that is an obstacle. But in serving the person you are brought closer together."

—January 3, 1972

"I think 1977 and 1978 will be the culmination of the fight between the two powers [God and Satan]. We want to save the whole world by conquering the satanic power and becoming the victors."

—January 9, 1972

"So we Christians must start from the point of having to go through difficulties and hardships in order to restore and indemnify God's original work. In order for us to do that—to love God—we must deny ourselves. So we must be ready to give away, give out our lives, lose our lives, deny ourselves, in order to obtain God's love. . . .

"We must struggle hard without sleeping, without eating, forgetting every worldly worry and going ahead with our goal and our vision. . . .

"Then who is going to save this country? We must be confident that we are those who can save this nation. . . .

"The history of our movement . . . started in 1960. We are entering the thirteenth year. The satanic power is doomed to decline, and by the year 1980, we are sure to see that the satanic sovereignty will have fallen.

"What I want you to do is to love God more than I have—love God whom I have loved, but more than I did. If you really love me, I want you to love God in place of me, more than I do him."

—December 9, 1972

"Evil does not come from God-centered motives or from other-centered motives, it comes from self-interest. . . .

"We can achieve the ideal world with the thought that for the interest of the whole world, we are willing to sacrifice our own nation. Unless there are those who want to sacrifice themselves for the sake of the whole world, the ideal world cannot be reached.

"In following me, I want you to resemble me. I want you to go through what I have gone through. In this group you have to go through this bitterness."

—January 24, 1973

"Jesus was forced to fail in carrying out his mission on the national level, even though he completed his mission on the individual level. So the one coming in his place has to accomplish what was left unaccomplished by Jesus—that is, he is going to accomplish things on every level, both spiritual and physical. . . .

"Once I have spoken I will make it a reality. I have got to make it. If we have money we can make a reality. You must not sleep much, rest much, eat much. You must work day and night to make this great task a reality—a success. By doing that you will shorten the path."

—January 30, 1973

"There is a long history of God having been deceived by the people, betrayed by the people—with much sadness and grief in His heart. Are you confident to have God trust you? Can your degree of loyalty or love of God eradicate all of man's history of betrayal?"

—March 1, 1973

"We have now an ultimate goal set before us. On the way, we need knowledge, we need position, we need power, wealth and everything—but the value of these must be entirely different from what we used to think. From now on we want to use all those things and all that we are for a greater cause. . . . Our goal is too bright and near—within our grasp, within our reach. . . . We are pioneers; we are God's heirs for the Great Cause. . . . Our goal is clear, only too clear: to establish the kingdom of God on earth. You may forget eating, but don't forget this. You may forget sleeping, but don't forget this goal. . . . We can do just anything to turn this world upside down, under God's will. We will let history prove it."

—March 22, 1973

"We have only a small number of people, but God relies on us. . . . We must be zealous and enthusiastic in raising money. We must be stingy in using money for ourselves, but generous in using the money for other people. . . . We are the visible incarnation of God; through us, God will be expressed; through us, God will be active.

"What we want to do is not just believe in God, but put God's teaching into practice, to make this world a world of love, the kingdom of God."

—April 1, 1973

121

"Every political and economic situation in every field can be solved based on the *Divine Principle.* . . .

"But when it comes to our age, we must have an automatic theocracy to rule the world. So we cannot separate the political field from the religious. God's loving people have to rule the world—that's logical."

—May 17, 1973

"Chastity and keeping pure is the greatest thing in our group. We have to revolutionize U.S. society. . . .

"If within seven years from now this cannot be realized, it may be prolonged to twenty-one more years. So, we must try our best to conclude our mission—in forty years at the latest."

—May 20, 1973

"God plans to make the twenty years between 1960 and 1980 a period of total advancement for the heavenly dispensation. . . . These three seven-year periods will end in 1981—twenty-one years. By these twenty-one years, we are restoring the entire fallen history in a horizontal way. . . .

"The eventual purpose of the restoration is to restore the Heavenly family. I urge you to reach out to your own parents and own people."

—July 1, 1973

"Anyone who is in the leader's position does not exist for himself. . . . You receive the message from Master. But if you don't act it out, the words will be valueless. . . .

"I am the central figure in the Unification Church, but I have never once thought of myself as the authoritative and most powerful one, being able to do anything I please to my members. . . .

"It is only some ten years ago that I began to wear gentlemen's suits. . . .

"My way of praying is very simple: Let me sacrifice myself for these people, and then let them sacrifice themselves for the rest of the world."

—November 9, 1973

"Communism is strongly systematized, but they are doing it at gunpoint, using the gun, the knife. We heavenly soldiers are doing it with bubbling and willing enthusiasm. Nobody is forcing you, except your own will, determination and joy."

—January 31, 1974

"Our church's past history in Korea, step by step, was really bloodshed, hard battle and continuous persecution. . . . He laid a spiritual foundation so we could move out of Korea into the worldwide dispensation. . . .

"The satanic power is mobilizing the Christian churches to come against us. . . .

"This is the road of the cross. Yes, I witness so much opposition outside and in each city it is intensifying. Actually, I want this. I am making the opposition a worldwide opposition so that we can make a worldwide unity. Then we can win by overcoming this oppositional unity. . . .

"You must draw God's power. With your power you can never make it. . . . You must live with me spiritually all the time. This is the secret of our movement. . . .

"The first thing we will begin with is prayer. Prayer is the beginning of our campaign."

—April 14, 1974

"God himself has dual essentialities, male and female—or masculine and femininity. . . .

"You must be more strongly drawn to God's love than your spouse's love. . . .

"In the history of restoration, God is seeking man, God is looking for man."

—August 4, 1974

"No, no one, including Reverend Moon, can say, 'I am the source of true life and love.' . . .

"So aren't you crazy, you young people who are just blossoming in life, many not even married, yet you are willing to die for the cause of God! Many people will point their finger at you and call you crazy and say Reverend Moon has ruined your life. Even then, are you determined to go on? . . .

"We say that we want to become saints and live sacred lives, but that life is not an easy one. There is no freedom in that life. You must give up your own will and live for God's will. . . .

"Sometimes I wish every Unification Church member including Bo Hi Pak would be kidnapped. I want you to be tested, to see how unchangeable you are. . . .

"We are the pioneers and will be remembered as the church's ancestors. . . .

"We're very different. Then why do they call you Moonies? It is . . . the resemblance of our minds and spirits. We are both determined to save the world, and nothing can detour us until we achieve the goal. . . .

"God may sacrifice the Unification Church in order to save the world. Are you ready for that? . . .

"I know there is great peril and chaos ahead for America. I can see it coming. I can read the signs. . . .

"We are proclaiming the liberation of God. We will liberate God from His sorrow. That is our goal."

—August 1, 1976

"Any man who says that he is the source of life and love cannot be trusted, not even Reverend Moon. . . .

"If you truly love me, then you will pray to become even stronger than Jesus, to be able to face even greater obstacles than Jesus might have faced."

—August 1, 1976

"I hereby proclaim that, culminating with the victory at Washington Monument, the first phase of the ministry that I initiated when I came to America in 1972 has been successfully concluded. . . . From today on, we are different people. From this time on you don't need my presence. From this day on we move to a new plateau, a new stage of our movement. . . .

"It is immaterial whether or not I can unify the world within my lifetime, for the work will go on and on, and I will continue to lead it, whether I am here on earth or in the spirit world. . . .

"Think ahead to 1980 . . . and what kind of victory you will have won by that year. By then the Unification Church will stand upon an invincible foundation."

—September 20, 1976

"Your parents sometimes come and oppose me, but contrary to their understanding I am raising their children to make them saints and historical people. . . .

"The greatest ideology has been revealed through me, and you know it. That is why I am destined to remain controversial until we change the world completely."

—December 5, 1976

"The year of 1977 is the year for a leap of success and great glory. The years of the dispensation up to 1976 have been for indemnity, for paying off the debts of the past. Now that a firm foundation has been erected completely, all we have to do in 1977 is expand on the horizontal level. . . .

"It is my great pleasure to proclaim this morning that after six thousand years of Biblical history the Unification

Church has achieved the cornerstone of the ideal family here on earth. . . .

"What is the definition of the ideal family? The ideal family possesses the eternal love of God. We have the mission to create the ideal family here on earth. . . .

"Now we have come to the era when we can physically construct the Kingdom of God here on earth by creating the family. This year we are going to concentrate on the construction of the ideal family and on this love of parents."

—January 1, 1977

"Almighty God, who is the creator of heaven and earth, and of mankind, is appearing to you directly in the forms of Mother and me, borrowing our images to work with you. . . .

"The spirit world could not function until the appearance of the Unification Church. . . .

"No, the source of power is not in me. It is in God. I only serve as a channel for that power to flow from Him to you. Our key to unlock the kingdom of God here on earth is this: you must make a relationship with me, feel a closeness and warmth of love for the True Parents and expand it to every corner of the earth.

"This year I declared as a motto of the year 1977: The Kingdom of God on earth and the Ideal Family."

—January 1, 1977

"Our young people must know why I have pushed them into such a miserable way of life. . . . If you listen to me, within several years' time all our dreams will become real. . . .

"Those who do not have an appetite of arduous, difficult tasks had better pack up now. . . . The countdown has started. Unless we lay a sufficient foundation in these two years, the free world will decline. In 1976, 1977, and 1978 we will pay indemnity for the cosmic dispensation. Truly the kingdom of heaven shall be a living reality here on earth. . . . We shall not be stopped."

—January 1, 1977

"Even I cannot be trusted 100 percent because of the innate nature of human weaknesses. You may not trust me 100 percent, but you must trust my teaching, my words 100 percent because they are not my own. They are God's words. How do you know I'm not the world's worst con man or swindler? You can only trust me by experiencing life together with me."

—January 2, 1977

"God can prolong restoration history if certain expectations do not occur right on schedule. God cannot use the same people or the same territory twice. The new Messianic mission will unfold in Asia. God will choose one homogeneous, united people, a single race which has a deep religious history and religious capability. . . .

"The victory of the Washington Monument Rally was the most significant event in human history. The spirit world was liberated; the barriers were broken and they no longer exist. Even if I pass away, the mission will not stop. . . .

"I am declaring to you that as of today, all the dispensational history of restoration has ended, has been completed. We will win God's territory back, inch by inch, until the year of 2000."

—February 23, 1977

The Author's Questions
and the Replies
of Sun Myung Moon

O the Lord is come, O the Lord is come!
In the East where the sun appears,
Land that is chosen of God.

—from a Unification Church song

As my letters with both the publishers and church
officials had specified, the climactic interview with Reverend Moon was planned and agreed to from the beginning.
When we came right down to the deadline, it was not easy
to arrange. Moon had given one interview before with
Newsweek, when they were planning their International
Edition cover story, but Reverend Moon's image of himself
is not to engage constantly in open interchange. His public
appearances, like the one at Madison Square Garden, are
quite different, as I will explain. Furthermore, I knew that,
with the conclusion of the Washington Monument rally,
Moon had announced an end even to such appearances as
these. But when the book manuscript was done in rough
draft, I went to New York City to conclude some interviews
I had missed in my other visits and to wait for the Moon
interview to be arranged. After much negotiation, this was
done, but it was also made quite clear that there would be
no more such interviews; this would be the last. Thus, the
occasion took on an added significance.

Officials would not show Moon the list of questions I had
submitted in advance. He does not work that way, they
said, and on reflection I think that is true. No one knew
exactly how long the interview would last or how many of

Left: The former New Yorker Hotel, now Unification Church World Mission Center. *Right:* From left to right, Bo Hi Pak, Neil Salonen, Frederick Sontag, and Sun Myung Moon during the author's nine-hour interview with Moon.

my questions I would be able to get over. As it turned out, we simply stayed at the lunch table and talked on until Moon sent out for dinner to be brought in, and then on even after the dishes were cleared away. Observers reported that Reverend Moon relaxed and spoke openly to me, as he does on few occasions I was told, and this was certainly my impression. The interview was a candid exchange beyond my ability to have predicted—and evidently no one else could have predicted this either. I wished at the time that I were a more skilled interviewer or that I had had more questions prepared or that I had had time to review his answers more fully for the additional questions they raised. But given the uncertainties about the interview and my own lack of skill in such matters, it still added up to as open a response as I could have hoped for. "He revealed himself to you," said one of the observers at the table, and so it seemed to me he did. Of course, Moon speaks in abstractions, as philosophers do, which makes it hard to pin him down to specifics.

This lengthy interview took place on Thursday, February 3, 1977, in New York City, in the former New Yorker Hotel, now Unification World Mission Center. We began at 12:30 with lunch and preliminary conversation. Mrs. Moon was present for lunch, in addition to the technical recording and transcribing staff. Bo Hi Pak, Mr. Moon's official translator, conducted the session. Neil Albert Salonen, president of the American church, was present most of the time. Young Whi Kim, president of the Korean church, audited the whole conversation. Considering his reputation for dress, Moon surprised everyone by appearing for the interview in a sport shirt (see cover photo). Evidently the conservative age is past, and this is the friendly sport-shirt era.

Six hours of formal interview dialogue were recorded and the whole occasion extended over nine hours. I had prepared forty-nine questions in advance. These grew out of the basic body of the book as I wrote it and out of the issues I have listed in chapter 7. My questions to him reflected the topics I thought the general public would like to have answered, and I was able to insert all but a few minor questions into our conversation. I have edited the 104-page transcript down to manageable size primarily by picking out key sentences. I have omitted elaborate and doctrinal statements which readers can find elsewhere.

Frederick Sontag:
People inside the church have heard many of your words, but the average person outside really has never heard you speak on the controversial matters. I've discovered one reason why having your own words is so important. Something true may be said, but it is said in such a way that it's interpreted differently by opposing sides. Many descriptions of the church are true, but they are put in a way that completely changes the outsider's understanding. This is why I've gone to such length to quote church members and nonchurch members in conversation. I hope this will be one virtue of my book. It allows the people to speak and to say what they want to in the way they would like to be interpreted.

Sun Myung Moon:
Yes, what you say is so true. This is why I am deeply grateful that a scholar like you has taken the time to research in depth both our movement and our critics alike and has tried to come up with an objective, fair appraisal. Most of the misunderstandings about our movement and me here in America are due to ignorance. So I am very happy to answer some of the questions you have.

As you probably know, I have given my life, my honor, my entire family, everything I have, into this movement. Unless I was certain I had something absolutely right, I wouldn't have done that. I know there is something real on my side, so anybody who joins me will not be a loser. I am not working at random or just on a whim. Our movement has a deep spiritual origin. It came into being at this particular time by a mandate of God. I have a divine guiding light. Even though many people think I am just doing things my own way, there is no such thing as my own way.

In a way, I am gratified to have such all-out negative publicity, or to be negatively interpreted by the American public. This testifies to the newness of my revelation. Every religious pioneer, including Jesus Christ, was persecuted by his contemporaries. But once people understand me, their turn can be dramatic like Saint Paul's. I knew from the beginning that when I came to America I would have to pass through tests and terrible tribulations. But the persecution and hostilities only make our members and me stronger. True religious movements prosper and flourish under tribulation.

Sontag:

If you feel that God elected Korea for a special role in the development of religion today, could you say a little more about why you think Korea is the place chosen for God's action in the present time?

Moon:

Korea has several very unique characteristics. First of all, the Korean people are a homogeneous, united people. Second, they are very religious. They naturally have a deep religious understanding. Third, they understand suffering. Throughout history, the Korean people have gone through tremendous ordeals and hardship. Under these conditions the Korean people have developed an undying spirit of loyalty and dedication.

These are the most important characteristics for a people to be chosen by God—because they match his own personality. Throughout history no one has suffered more than God. He has suffered because his own children fell away from him. Ever since the Fall, God has been working tirelessly for the restoration of mankind. People do not know this brokenhearted aspect of God. In order to really understand God's suffering and to establish a rapport with him, the three characteristics I mentioned before are very important. The chosen people of Israel had these characteristics two thousand years ago. Today Korea has much in common with God's heart. From their own experience of suffering and tragedy, Koreans can readily understand God's sorrow and broken heart. They can readily respond to the call of God.

In this respect, we can also answer why God has chosen me as his instrument at this time of the Providence. The same things can be said about me. I have an unchanging will; I am deeply religious, and I, too, have been tested and strengthened by tribulations and hardships. When God revealed himself and his mission to me, I could readily understand his heart. I couldn't help but weep. I determined then to give my life completely to ease his broken heart. It has been my honor and privilege since then to carry his sorrow on my shoulders. My every action is to liberate God from his sorrow.

Sontag:

Could you say a little about the religious situation as you became aware of it in Korea when you started your mission?

Moon:

Actually, the preparation of Korea as the birthplace for this new spiritual movement was very adequate back in 1945. For example, Christianity was flourishing. The depth of Christian faith in Korea was extraordinary at that time. Also, there were many spiritual groups who received prophecies about the coming of a new spiritual movement. They were groups that could have served well in the role of John the Baptist. But why didn't these groups testify to us once the new movement had finally come?

There is always human responsibility involved. Two thousand years ago the people lacked the humility necessary to accept Jesus. This was again lacking in Korea. Acceptance was not there, simply because of arrogance. The existing churches rejected our new spiritual movement. I had to start from the role of John the Baptist in order to lay the initial foundation upon which I could construct my own mission.

Sontag:

If you take traditional theology and measure the *Divine Principle* against it, it is heresy. There's something new there. I wonder, without trying to appraise it, what you would say about the role of such new revelations from God. Do they represent a departure?

Moon:

First of all, Christianity itself, in its development for two thousand years has departed considerably from the original will or dispensation of God. In two thousand years, Christianity has broken into hundreds of denominations; it has been divided by sectarianism. Because Christians have created their own barriers, they are blocking their own goals. This is the most important reason that God needs man to have an absolutely new and totally fresh outlook. God needs a new vision of life to be instilled in the minds of the people. Unless there is a fresh, new approach, God sees no way for his original, ultimate goal to be accomplished. The *Divine Principle* is that new revelation. The people who join this movement find a new vision and new spiritual power. These people have become the fundamental strength behind this new revolution for the permanent establishment of Christendom.

Second, and most important, our movement stresses the salvation of the world as the primary goal. Our personal salvation becomes secondary. We are willing to sacrifice ourselves for the sake of the world and humanity. In contrast, many conventional church-goers are concerned about their own places in heaven and their own eternal lives. Actually, the teaching of a sacrificial spirit is nothing new. This was the fundamental teaching of Jesus Christ. Jesus came to the world to save the world, not to save himself. However, Christianity somehow lost the essential vigor and the very spirit of Jesus; his purpose has been turned around. I merely came to refresh the spirit of Jesus Christ. The concept is old, but somehow has dimmed. We are now revitalizing it, making it real. I always teach that the Unification Church itself is not a goal. I must serve as God's instrument to bring about the salvation of the world. This is the only justification for the existence of the Unification Church. There are enough churches already, but the world still needs salvation.

The Unification Church is very aggressive in this vision. We venture where the sins are, in order to eliminate them. We tackle sin instead of shying away from it. For example, in the case of my Watergate statement, the wisest thing I could have done was to shy away from the situation. That was an unpopular cause. But instead of shying away from it, I plunged right in. Why? Because I know the religious leaders have to speak out on the fundamental issue of the day and try to pose solutions.

This is why the Unification Church acts upon many things that others cannot understand. We have a different outlook. We may not benefit by taking certain actions at a particular moment, but we look at everything from a worldwide, long-range point of view. We act for the sake of the nation, the world, and posterity. When I see that a certain goal must be obtained in order to benefit the future of mankind, then we commit ourselves to it, even though it is an unpopular move at the time and appears to be a sure loss. We suffer greatly because of it, but we still do it. It is adventurous and very bold. Even though we may look foolish sometimes in the eyes of man, as long as our action is righteous in the eyes of God we go ahead with it.

Sontag:

You move into the centers of secular life and that creates controversy. But do you see a danger that, in attempting to work in these centers to bring the world back to God, you might yourself be trapped in the mess that you're trying to clean up?

Moon:

This is a religious movement; we do everything with religious conviction. Therefore, instead of being taken over by the situation and becoming victims of circumstance, we are bound to come out as winners even though we may have to pay a price. Under my leadership, the Unification Church often commits itself to impossible tasks rather than ordinary ones. But we will never leave a task undone or only half-way finished. I would like to win the reputation that once the Unification Church moves, it will fulfill and accomplish.

The beauty of our Washington Monument rally was that, while the leader was a man from Korea who belongs to the yellow race, people of all races, coming even from Europe, Africa, South America, India, were all working together there. God sees real beauty in the multicolor harmony of the truly international family we are striving to build.

Sontag:

There is a significance to your city and state tours and the Madison Square Garden, Yankee Stadium, and Washington Monument rallies. I think these are very little understood in the outside world. Could you say something about your view of the significance of these events?

Moon:

I came to America primarily to declare the New Age and new truth. Whether the people accept me at once or not, it is my God-given duty to speak. This is why God appeared to me and told me to go to America to speak the truth. I hesitated because I didn't even speak English, but still he commanded me to go. Through my cross-country tours I somewhat fulfilled this mission of declaration. During the Day of Hope tour, I visited all fifty states. These were not just evangelical meetings in the ordinary sense. They had great providential significance, great spiritual meaning.

I do not know how much insight or understanding you have about the spirit world, but it is so real in our movement. Our movement is not just a horizontal movement; it is vertical. Everything we do is reflected in the spirit world, and we reflect the spirit world as well; both worlds work together in our movement. From a horizontal point of view, perhaps there seems to be no meaning in certain of our actions. Sometimes we may seem to waste time, waste money and energy. But sometimes what we do here on earth helps in the spirit world. Also, we do certain things to set conditions so that the power of the spirit will pour down on the earth. The established churches or religious organizations in this country are generally declining, overwhelmed by secular thoughts, secular culture. But the Unification Church is different; we don't feel any decline of spirit in our movement. We are pioneers; we are like a volcano erupting.

I am sure you have heard from some of my speeches after the Washington Monument rally that now the time has come for the entire spirit world to cooperate. It is ready to come down to assist our movement. As you know, on October 4, 1976, I declared the Day of the Victory of Heaven after the Washington Monument rally. A new era has dawned, and the barriers between religions in the spirit world have literally been broken down. Unity was formed and spirits are really assaulting the earth. This phenomenon is happening in various ways.

Sontag:

How do you see your own role in relation to the role of Jesus?

Moon:

One of my most important revelations is that Jesus Christ did not come to die. He came to this world to consummate his messianic mission given by God, which is the establishment of the kingdom of God here on earth. Through his crucifixion, however, Jesus gave himself as a sacrifice for the faithlessness of the world, and by his resurrection, he established spiritual salvation. This is the teaching of the *Divine Principle*. Complete salvation, which is physical as well as spiritual, was the ultimate purpose and intended goal of God for mankind at the time of Jesus. That mission was not totally accomplished. We must realize, however, that this was not because of any fault on the part of Jesus Christ. Rather it was because of the rejection by the people. This point is greatly misunderstood today. The Second Coming was predicted because the mission was not totally accomplished in the first. Therefore, a messianic crusade is destined to begin here on earth in order to consummate the will of God. The work of the Unification Church and my mission is to proclaim the coming of the Messianic Age.

From the Christian church's point of view, my teaching, the new revelation, is not only extraordinary, but revolutionary. I can understand why Christians call us heretics. But most important, who will God call a heretic? From God's point of view, my revelation is deeply orthodox. If the mission of Jesus Christ had been completely fulfilled in his time, then there would be no need for the birth of the Unification Church. My mission would not be needed.

Sontag:

The goal of your church is to unite all churches and to produce the unified family. Yet in Korea and now here, you have built up such tension; you have begun by separating families and rousing the opposition of churches. Do you see that as an irony? How will you move to accomplish your goal?

Moon:

It truly is an irony. However, from the spiritual point of view, a great blessing is coming to those families because their sons and daughters are working for this new messianic mission of the Unification Church. Furthermore, this is a heavenly emergency on a worldwide scale. When a national emergency comes, a soldier leaves his wife and children behind temporarily and goes out to defend his country. From God's point of view, these children have been summoned for the greatest heavenly emergency and a most glorious mission. The incredible grievances and complaints come only because people do not see this spiritual aspect.

I have never divided families or broken homes. Actually, in many cases, I have restored families and united them in happiness. I have received numerous thank-you letters from grateful parents. In some other cases, families are trying to blame me for damage that was done long before.

Whether someone joins our church or not is not a matter of age, or being a child or parent; it's a matter of the magnetic power of the truth. Anybody who touches the truth has to be ignited. When you touch the most total, brilliant truth of all, you cannot settle for some semitruth. The parent-child relationship is beautiful and full of love. However, let's say a child tastes an even greater love than he is experiencing at home with his parents. Let's say he experiences something far greater than his ordinary family relationships. The child then feels he must go to the source of that greater love in order to be spiritually satisfied.

When people detect this life force, they just cannot help but be drawn in by its magnetic strength. Spiritually speaking, God's new truth has come as a source of life and light. Jesus Christ was the Prince of Peace, and he indeed came to bring true peace. Yet he said, "Do not think that I have come to bring peace on earth. I have not come to bring peace but a sword."

Do these words contradict Jesus as the Prince of Peace? No. We must understand that Jesus came for true, eternal peace. To establish such peace, a fundamental change in human life was necessary. A revolution of man was inevitable.

To attain this true peace, Jesus first sought to bring about a revolution of man. In this sense he came for war. He fully intended to bring about a fundamental change in man, in society, in the nation and the world. Because of this, when he taught he met with a violent reaction. Established societies always resist any major change. Jesus was persecuted and finally crucified.

Today our world still needs drastic change in order to become God-centered. I came to call for that change. The *Divine Principle* will bring about a revolution of man. The power of this truth is touching millions of human lives and is igniting hundreds of thousands of them. It will bring about the true, lasting unification of the family of man and the world. Yet, we are met with tension and resistance. If we look to the lesson of history, however, we can see that this is the normal, inevitable pattern for the pioneering days of any serious spiritual movement.

In Korea, in our pioneering days, many housewives came to our church. In early days there seemed to be more women members attracted to the truth. They are more religious, I guess. But they received tremendous persecution at home. Some husbands hated the fact that their wives went to church, so they took extreme measures to embarrass their wives. Sometimes they would cut their hair; they would shave it off so they couldn't go outside because people would laugh. But these persons would still come to the church at midnight to pray and worship. They would put small handkerchiefs on to hide their heads and still come. Sometimes the scarves blew off, but they didn't mind. They would just rather come to church even if humiliated. Some persons were deprived of all their clothes, but they came with rags. Amazing. The power that draws people to the source of life is amazing. Incredible. It is because of these—in a way, crazy—acts, that Reverend Moon was subjected to such unwarranted persecution in the early days. Those people were so drawn to the church. People would say, "Reverend Moon must be brainwashing them, giving some tonic or pills to make them crazy." That kind of persecution came, not only here in America but in Korea, too.

Sontag:

As you know, the training and conversion methods of your church are hotly debated. I wonder if you see anything that's essentially different from other evangelical or monastic movements in the way that people are trained, in the way in which converts are brought to your church.

Moon:

You have been in many centers of the Unification Church. You know as well as I what we are doing is a process of education. We talk to people and bring them to hear the *Divine Principle.* All we do is teach the *Divine Principle.* We have workshops, but what is a workshop? It is simply the teaching of the *Divine Principle.* Furthermore, no doors are locked and anyone can leave anytime from our centers. But people stay to hear the teaching. The proselytizing and witnessing methods basically are not new. They are not different from those of the conventional Christian churches. What is different is the truth that we have, the truth of the *Divine Principle.*

Another point I would like to make is that many people outside the church think that American youth are brought to me, and I hypnotize them somehow. Somehow I brainwash them and make them members. Actually, I have never even given one *Divine Principle* lecture to any newcomer. They never come to meet me until they have already become members. Sometimes they may come to the Sunday service and hear me speak, but that is all. Whether I am here or not doesn't make the Unification Church win or lose members. There is the truth, the *Divine Principle,* and anybody can learn and teach the Principle. It awakens people to a deeper understanding of the work of God and a more fulfilling personal relationship with God.

Many members of the mobile fund-raising teams have never met me. The people learn the Principle, become strong members, and dedicate themselves to the cause. They do this not because of my personal influence or because I tell them they must do it or be cursed. Many people outside the church almost seem to think there is some high-powered gadget attached to the fund raisers which I control. It is nonsense.

Sontag:

Outsiders seem to detect a sense of conspiracy about the church and its activities. Why does it arouse this suspicion about its activities?

Moon:

You know the Unification Church does not have any secrets. Many people think it is surrounded by secrets, like some sort of super CIA-type operation. It's amazingly ironic, because our operation is completely open. I do not have anything to hide. Too many times people will not come to the church and find out the truth for themselves. They are always welcome; we operate in the open. Then why does an atmosphere "shrouded with conspiracy" come about?

The truth is that our adversaries, those who feel threatened by me or the Unification Church, spread these rumors. The Christian churches are fearful. They feel their establishment will be taken over, their land and structures may be taken over; their young people may become members of the Unification Church. So, in fear of losing their young people they are very defensive. In order to defend themselves, the best thing, as has always been the case throughout history, is to paint the worst possible picture of their opponent's doctrine and method of operation.

The amount of criticism and persecution our church and I have received in the last thirty years is so incredible that I have to be thankful to God that finally we are established and successful today. Without the power of God we would have been annihilated many times over.

Today, there are many people who feel threatened by me and feel they must somehow eliminate me. They feel I am such a menace to their prosperity, their future, and their children that they have gone to the extreme of saying, "We must do something to eliminate Reverend Moon and exterminate the Unification Church." I have no animosity toward those who are trying to destroy me. My job, my God-given mission, is to liberate them from hate and fear, to give them light to guide them into eternal salvation. We want to lead them into being the beneficiaries of the ultimate blessing from God.

Sontag:

Your control of property and money is a very controversial item concerning the church. I wonder if you would comment on how you see the control and use of wealth as necessary to the church's program and how you view its control?

Moon:

The holdings we have in New York and all over the world are part of the blessing from God. All material things were created by God as a blessing or a gift to his children. But

138

because of the Fall of Man, men and women have not become God's true sons and daughters. The time will come for God's own children to be restored into God's lineage, as direct heirs entitled to master and utilize all the things of creation for the glory of God. I do not condemn material things as satanic. The deciding factor is the man who controls them and uses them. If your motivation is absolutely God-centered, absolutely unselfish, then the material things are there for you to utilize for the benefit of humanity.

Let us for a moment examine what kind of property holdings we have. As you know, our church has acquired the old New Yorker Hotel on Eighth Avenue and Thirty-fourth Street. This gigantic two-thousand-room hotel was lying dead in the midst of Manhattan. When I first looked inside it, I could not believe my eyes. It was a total wreck. It looked as though it had been bombed. It looked like Seoul after the Korean War. I could not understand how such a disaster area could be in the very heart of New York City.

We bought and are restoring this building into full life. We are presently using it as our movement's World Mission Headquarters. The kingdom of God is the kingdom of use. It's like resurrecting a dead body and bringing it to the use of God. The New Yorker is typical of many of our real-estate purchases. We purchase dead, wasted property and restore it to full use for God and humanity. We purchased the defunct former Columbia University Club, gave it new life, and are now using it as our U.S. church headquarters. We also purchased the Manhattan Center. It used to be New York's most famous opera house, but that once beautiful center was left to decay for several decades. Now our young people have been working to renovate it over a period of several months. It has become a main sanctuary for our church.

We have most recently purchased the old Tiffany Building. At one time it was a symbol of America's graciousness and opulence. This building has become our *News World* Newspaper Company headquarters. We also took over the decayed Lofts Candy Factory and are using it for our church publications department. We also took over the vacated Christian Brothers Seminary, which had been decaying for five years in Barrytown, and its 270 acres of land. We rebuilt it into our Unification Theological Seminary. We have bought several hundred acres of land in Tarrytown, New York, as the site for a future university. These kinds of purchases are where the bulk of our money has gone.

All in all, who will be the beneficiaries of these? Ultimately, the general public and, of course, our members and their children. We do it as our service to God and humanity. I should think New York City would welcome our improvements if for no other reason than that they beautify the city and raise the value of the neighborhoods. What we are doing is truly refreshing, and once the American people truly understand, they will welcome it.

Our movement has the vitality, energy, and determination necessary to restore the old pioneering spirit of America. We are not only striving to restore the dying Christian spirit and the founding spirit of this nation, but we are also in reality restoring dying buildings and wasted land into productivity and a kind of paradise.

New York's Eighth Avenue could be called the Avenue of the Prostitutes. We want to restore Eighth Avenue into the Avenue of Heaven and Beauty. Our goal is one of restoration both spiritually and physically. As you might know, during our Yankee Stadium campaign we initiated the America-the-Beautiful program. Our young people, by the thousands, cleaned up the dirty streets of New York City every morning. We hope to make this a national program. Everyone must participate to make it work. Americans must be proud of the beautiful heritage and country which God has blessed them with.

Newspapers keep misrepresenting the situation by saying that I am getting rich. They don't say it directly, but through nuance they imply that I am storing up wealth in a Swiss bank somewhere. Our people here with me know better. I own nothing personally. Our movement owns everything and properly manages and uses everything for the task of building the Kingdom here on earth.

There are many suspicions about the source of our funds nowadays. Some people think it comes from the Korean CIA, the Korean government, or any number of places. But the whole truth is that the money comes only from the efforts of the Unification Church members. This money is the result of the blood and sweat of those members. Sacrificial duty brought it. Our members are the first to laugh when anybody says our young people are becoming robots, that they are manipulated. They know what they are doing and why.

It's my desire and goal to leave something here in America. I am not here permanently. Many people around the world come to America trying to get something. I am one man who came trying to give everything I have to America. Yet, I am more criticized.

Sontag:

The political involvement of the church is highly controversial too. Would you comment on just how you see your own and the church's relationship to political and secular authority?

Moon:

Our movement is basically a spiritual and religious one. We are destined to change the world because our goal is not just spiritual but physical as well. It involves everybody. How shall we do it? Not by military take-over or violence, but through a process of education, particularly education of the leadership of nations. This is where the Unification Church and I get involved. We go out and witness about God not only to the multitude of people on the streets, but also to those people who could lead the country toward God. Our desire is to put new life into their hearts, that they might become God-centered leaders. This is our process for changing the world.

I do not think in terms of taking over the power or government of a nation. I am not ambitious to become a senator or the head of state of this or any other country. But as a messenger of God, my responsibility is to relay the message of God to the people who actually run the country and the society, to those who can actually influence the nation.

During the Watergate incident people said, "Oh, this is a political organization; they support Nixon. Their motivation is political." However, what did we actually do? We organized the Prayer and Fast Committee for a national emergency, and we prayed and fasted a lot. Many members of the Unification Church fasted three days and even seven days consecutively for the nation. We prayed on the Capitol Building's steps in an overnight vigil. We prayed in front of the White House and at the Lincoln Memorial. We prayed for congressmen, for senators, and for the President. I remember President Lincoln issued a proclamation to call the entire nation to confess its national sins and to pray for mercy and forgiveness during a time of emergency.

I felt that the Watergate was a national emergency. It was a moral crisis, a national sin. While American soldiers were dying in Vietnam, the people at home were deeply wounded internally and divided. They were losing faith in everything and couldn't support those abroad. I felt that the healing grace needed could come only from God, and the power of prayer could invoke it. I wanted to call this nation to its knees in repentance. I hoped the President would issue a proclamation again, as Lincoln had, calling for

141

national prayer. Our movement wanted to set an example, and we did. I wanted to awaken the conscience of America. Is this a political action?

If you read my Watergate statement, you will find it is a genuine sermon filled with the same spirit as the Sermon on the Mount: Forgive, love, unite. These three words truly express the essence of Christian teaching and are far from any political ambition.

Sontag:

I wonder if you would say a little about the development of your own prayer life. It seems to me that the prayer life within the church is something unique, and many members comment that they learned to pray only within the church.

Moon:

First of all, I believe that prayer is the most powerful thing. It can change the impossible into the possible. Secondly, in the Unification Church I emphasize prayer but prayer in a different manner. Don't pray for yourself—this is my teaching. Pray for your mission; pray for others; pray so that your prayer can reach God as a comforting word.

Sontag:

The doctrine of True Parents, I think, is much misunderstood. I wonder if you would say something about the relationship between True Parents and one's natural parents and the kind of obligation the child has to both.

Moon:

Parents is the word used to designate a person's father and mother, those who gave him life. Our concept of *True Parents* refers to the rebirth of an individual. The true you is spiritual. Our real selves are invisible, yet that is what was corrupted. Therefore all people are destined to be reborn. Ultimately God is the True Parent. But because God is spirit and invisible, he creates a central person or persons through whom mankind can receive God's teaching and experience rebirth. These are the True Parents. This concept of True Parents does not disregard the natural parent at all.

Since the fall of Adam and Eve, the work of God has been the reorganization of the human family. The human family stems from fallen Adam and Eve, and God cannot accept the family as it is. It must go through a reformation or rebirth process. This was the teaching of Jesus Christ even two thousand years ago. Therefore, we need God and God-ordained True Parents. Your natural parents give you physical life and love you, and raise you with the best moral principles they can. True Parents give you spiritual life. The term Holy Father has been used for years to indicate a representative of God in church life. The concept *True Parents* should not, therefore, seem so strange.

Adam and Eve were supposed to be the True Parents of mankind in God's plan. When they failed, God intended Jesus to be the True Parent of mankind. When he was crucified on the cross, God promised another messiah. He is coming to consummate the ideal of God-centered True Parents. He will generate a new family of God through restoring the family unit under God's ideal. When we have True Parents of God, we can all become true brothers and sisters.

Sontag:

Then after the spiritual rebirth, what becomes of the relation and obligation of the child to his natural parents?

Moon:

His natural parents certainly remain his parents, and their family relationship will never change. After spiritual rebirth, however, one is related to the true family of God, and is responsible to restore his own natural parents, brothers, and sisters, and relatives to God's family, too. This makes an eternal relationship with God possible for those you love most. The true family's relationship is eternal, whereas an earthly family's is only temporal. Therefore, one needs to make both relationships possible within his natural family, thereby bringing complete restoration to his family. Mankind's ultimate fulfillment here on earth is to become true sons and daughters of God.

(Tea break. Ginseng tea is brought in.)

Sontag:

One other benefit of my trip to Korea was that I learned to like ginseng tea. I didn't like it before I went to Korea, but now I do. So I had a conversion experience in Korea!

Col. Pak:

Even though Reverend Moon created the ginseng tea factory, he was not a believer in it at first. He had a conversion experience to ginseng too. He began to enjoy the honeyed ginseng root. Reverend Moon says by taking that honeyed ginseng root regularly, it gives tremendous energy and vitality.

Sontag:

Is that the source of Reverend Moon's vitality?

Col. Pak:

Yes, God-given vitality and honeyed ginseng, that is a double guarantee now!

Moon:

In the morning, for example, on a Sunday I speak for

143

several hours. I take just one honeyed ginseng root in the morning, and I can talk until noon. I don't feel any fatigue or hunger. It's amazing. Particularly during middle-age, and I'm afraid we are both along there now, middle-age and above.

Neil Albert Salonen:

When we were in Korea, some of the Japanese leaders of the ginseng tea trading company said, "Under Father's direction we need two religions. We need *Divine Principle* for the spirit and ginseng tea for the body. We should have a ginseng tea religion!"

(Much laughter.)

Sontag:

I must warn Reverend Moon against laughing, because I talked to the psychiatrist in Boston who claims to be an expert on deprogramming. He told me that the sure sign a member is being deprogrammed successfully is that his sense of humor returns. So Reverend Moon mustn't laugh too much or he will deprogram himself!

(Laughter. End of tea break.)

Sontag:

As the church grows and spreads and becomes more successful and leaves its pioneering days, do you foresee a problem keeping your pioneering spirit alive?

Moon:

Our pioneering spirit will continue and remain alive. Until God's goal is reached, no one can really rest or relax. Just becoming a Christian is not our goal. My goal is the salvation of the world, and that's not even the end of it. We must liberate even God and the entire spirit world. The Unification Church is probably the first movement to describe God as suffering. In this respect our goal is total liberation: liberation of the sorrow of God.

Partial success is not really success. Our goal is set so high that we can in no way easily relax or be contented. I could very well say to our members, "You know, I worked hard enough for thirty years. Don't you think that's long enough for me to retire and relax and have a little fun now?" However, this kind of thinking does not even come into my mind. Why? Because I am always in the forefront of the pioneering spirit to further the goal.

Actually, I don't blame those people who call us heretics. We are indeed heretics in their eyes because the concept of our way of life is revolutionary: We are going to liberate God. We are going to liberate Jesus Christ. We are going to liberate them from sorrow, from brokenheartedness. Who in history has ever uttered such things? We not only say it, but we live it.

My concept of serving God is indeed revolutionary. God understands laughter, but more importantly, he understands sorrow and suffering. He has the aching heart of the parent when he looks down on suffering humanity. He wants the suffering to stop; as any parent. He wants happiness for his child. Let's say Jesus Christ is at the right hand of God. I am saying: Let us not only liberate this human world from sin, but liberate also the broken heart of God, the sorrow of Jesus. Do you think Jesus will say, "God, that man is wrong; take him away. We don't need his help. He is a blasphemer. I am the Truth, and I am the Life, and nobody can come to you but by me"? Would Jesus criticize me like that for trying to do his work?

No, even Jesus will say, "God, bless him. His work must be successful. The consummation of his work will be the consummation of my own mission. Therefore, his success is my success; his success is your success. God, please help him; please go down and inspire Reverend Moon and let him accomplish as much as he can in his lifetime."

The concept of judgment in Christian churches is grossly wrong. God is love; he condemns no one. But people do reap the consequences of what they sow. People who sow a selfish life here on earth will reap hell thereafter. But this is not the result of the condemnation of God. One cannot reap heaven if he lives and acts against God. God is a God of love; by having humanity suffering in hell, his heart is aching. He cannot enjoy this. God's desire is to ultimately liberate even hell.

Here in the world of flesh, we can leap ahead with great accomplishments through our actions. Our earthly life is a one-time opportunity. Let's say you live one hundred years here on earth. This is your opportunity to lay the foundation for your eternal life. Compared to eternity your hundred years on earth are less than the flash of a second. You must invest this one hundred years for God and humanity. Don't live just for yourself, for the moment. You will find much greater happiness if you give your one hundred years unselfishly for God; then God will reward you with eternity in heaven.

Sontag:

What problems do you see for the church and this work when you are no longer alive to lead it? How will the members respond to your absence?

Moon:

I have consummated my personal mission here on earth.

145

Therefore, whether I remain here on earth or whether I am taken to the spirit world doesn't make any difference. Our movement has laid a firm foundation. It exists here in the human level, but it is spiritually established; its root is God and the spirit world. On this foundation the movement will never fail. It will go on without me and the kingdom of God shall become a reality here on earth.

Sontag:

I want to know if you see any danger of the church drifting toward becoming just another church among many. What can happen is that people who are establishment-oriented gain control and then empire-ambition begins to dominate.

Moon:

This is the fundamental difference between the existing churches and the Unification Church. Ours is not a denomination but a movement of unification. Therefore, this movement will not cease in its revolutionary zeal or its pioneering task until the ultimate goal of establishing the kingdom of God here on earth is physically accomplished and God is able to take great comfort and joy after his six thousand biblical years of suffering.

We really could not become just an institutionalized established church. This is really a movement, and it will not settle down until the movement is no longer necessary.

Sontag:

Do you feel that each of your projected stages has succeeded? Is there any notion in your mind to revise the program in the future, or has the movement really met each stage as you originally envisaged it? Will the timetable be revised?

Moon:

No, no revision. Every timetable set has been obtained. I feel we have attained all the planned goals so far.

My coming to America was precisely on schedule; the next three and a half years' work was precisely on schedule. Yankee Stadium was on schedule, and the Washington Monument rally was on schedule. Now, the two-year program which I started for 1977 and 1978 for total evangelism throughout the country is also on schedule.

Sontag:

As I understand it, the original *Divine Principle* was oral in nature. The earliest disciples told me that they heard it in sermon form, and the disciples in Pusan said they were with you when the Principles were finally written down. In contrast to the very earliest writing, the present book is more elaborate, more detailed. Do you foresee the possibility again of any change, elaboration, addition, or subtraction of the present *Divine Principle* book? Is its form fixed now?

Moon:

The expression of parts of the Principle here and there have been greatly experimented with. But from the very beginning to the end, the basic content of the revelation has never altered. For example, in "The Principles of Creation," "The Fall of Man," and "The Mission of Jesus," the central ideas have never changed. I know there are difficulties in expressing certain concepts and ideas of our philosophy, so one of my projects, which will take a great deal of time and effort, is once again to standardize the Principle myself and leave it to history. This job remains to be done.

The *Divine Principle* is not the kind of truth that you have a conference about, and if people do not like it, you can change it. That will never happen. Also, there is a much greater area of truth yet to be revealed. I have already received the revelation, but I am purposely reserving certain truths to be revealed in future days.

Sontag:

So you do feel that there will be future revelation, that revelation is not closed.

Moon:

The *Divine Principle* is not a philosophy, not a theory; it is a principle. It is an unchanging truth of God. Once that truth is revealed, then that principle must be lived, acted upon. At least a foundation for its accomplishment must be laid. Then Satan cannot invade. When a person is completely united with the truth, then Satan cannot take him away from God. For instance, if God and Adam and Eve had been completely united with truth, then there would have been no room for Satan to infiltrate. Truth must become incarnate. It must be lived or fulfilled within a living person. Otherwise it can be taken away and misused by Satan. This is why I do not reveal truth until the conditions are all met or the truth is embodied to a certain point. In a way then, the *Divine Principle*, this new revelation, is the documentary of my life. It is my own life experience. The *Divine Principle* is in me, and I am in the *Divine Principle*.

Sontag:

Many outside the church feel that every member is personally loyal to Reverend Moon as an individual, but when I talk to members, their statement and direction is always toward the Principle. Would you agree that the loyalty of the people is toward the Principle? The two are

connected because you are the bringer of the Principle, the revealer, the source. Is that an accurate expression?
Moon:

It is a very, very important question you ask. Many people say I am just a revealer of the truth, an instrument, but I also live it, embody it. Therefore, the only way people can understand me or my actions is through the Principle. Only through knowing and studying the Principle can they understand. This is why the more the members study the Principle, the more they understand me and the more loyal they become. The two are one and the same. But in our movement, no one yet understands God 100 percent.

Sontag:

You are often accused of being authoritarian and even dictatorial and militaristic. What would you say about your own sense of authority and how you exercise it? How would you express your own authority in relationship to members?

Moon:

Actually, anybody who really knows the *Divine Principle* would not take it that way. This is only the external appearance. After just one glance someone might say that I am authoritarian. But actually, let's think about God. You could say God is a dictator. He has no congress to report to, and he is not elected. But nobody calls God a dictator because he is love. Love is stronger than any authority. So when outsiders look only at my authority, they may consider me a dictator. But they totally miss the point. I am a parent to the members. Parents love children, not govern them. God loves, not governs. In the Unification Church, if you miss that spiritual quality of love, God's love, then you could describe the Unification Church as the worst kind of hell.

Sontag:

Why do you think that most of the world, and surely the public press, miss the spiritual side of the church and also, particularly, the spiritual side of your nature?

Moon:

They seem to deliberately refuse to see that side. That may be the major cause. It's as though they have already drawn their conclusions and are only trying to pick out supportive evidence for their conclusions. However, the many people who come to know us closely see that there is a tremendous bond and tie of warmth and love in our church, and that it emanated from God through me. We are being attacked all the time, and yet we are always winning and gaining success. It's an amazing principle, being attacked and yet gaining.

In the last year, 1976, the entire world took a position to oppose me. In every nation there was controversy. I wanted to expedite that controversy, so I sent out missionaries to 120 nations. Why? I was putting up lightning rods in every nation so that they were exposed to world persecution. The greater the persecution, the faster the satanic world will lose power. This is heavenly strategy, but who understands this strategy? The day will come, however, when they will truly know the Unification Church and me. The day will come when the truth will be known and the message of love will be taught. On that day, their regret will be deep.

Sontag:

You were talking about the way in which you receive attack. You don't yourself attack, but the interesting thing is that people reverse this. Outside, people are very fearful because they think the movement will resort to a militaristic posture and that you will command your members to go out with guns. What do you say about condoning force or violence to attain your goals?

Moon:

It's been God's principle never to attack first. God never attacks first. Evil and Satan always take initiative and try to destroy, but the heavenly side has the responsibility to defend itself. I preach our movement as essentially nonviolent and nonmilitaristic. Our movement has the greatest weapon—if you use that word—truth. We also have the greatest target: the human heart. Truth can change the human heart, and then that person is totally changed. Since his motivation is changed, every action and plan changes. That's the basic way we plan to conquer this world of evil, by using the word. We are conquerors by love, conquerors by truth, but not by violence, not by weapons.

Right now, with the threat of the Third World War, the question of whether there will truly be any hot war or not depends on human responsibility. But regardless of whether there is a war, the reality is that there is a confrontation between two worlds, one representing the side of Satan, the other representing the side of God. Communism is trying to take the world by force. But God will take the world by love. We must become the embodiment of this love.

Sontag:

What the press protests so often is the use of deception by members in fund raising and the use of "front" organizations by the church. Would the church ever condone this, and what reason would there be to conceal the church's activities?

Moon:

I emphasize honesty, purity, and unselfishness as the principal code of our members. Honesty comes first, particularly between God and man. Our Principle teaches that man's dishonesty brought about the separation between God and man. Even though our members may think they will invite more hostile persecution, I emphasize that they must present themselves as the ambassadors of God and tell people who they are first.

A member must say that he is a member of the Unification Church and that he is the follower of Sun Myung Moon. If he doesn't have the courage to say it, he is not worthy of me. I tell them it's wrong not to speak out for fear of bringing greater persecution to themselves, because that greater persecution will bring equally greater blessing. If they try to shy away from persecution, actually they are missing the whole blessing. Some local leaders may have tried to be expedient, but they didn't have any bad motivation. I can understand why such things may have happened in the face of persecution, but I do not condone such action.

The term *front organization* is not our word; it is a word that the media use. We do have many organizations, but not "front" organizations. They each have legitimate purposes to serve humanity in various ways. We have the International Cultural Foundation; we have clinics, paramedical teams, businesses. We have the Professors World Peace Academy. Each organization exists because there are necessary projects to fulfill. Each one has its own distinct function. Our movement deals with the reality of the world. Ultimately, we want to serve all human needs. After all, our goal is the establishment of the kingdom of God on earth. We are not shying away from the world. Our movement is a movement of action, not just of meditation.

Sontag:

Reverend Moon, you are often accused of teaching one thing publicly and teaching some different, stronger doctrine to your followers in private. This is what many people suspect. What could be the basis for this? This is widely felt, I might say.

Moon:

I am never afraid of speaking out in public. The words of God can have no compromise. All the prophets in history have spoken out boldly, and so do I. As a matter of fact, in public speeches, not only at Yankee Stadium or the

Washington Monument, but at public speeches to the members (which anybody can come hear as you did), sometimes I speak with extraordinary candor. Sometimes I speak in the strongest terms in public. Why? Because I want it to register. I do not speak as a diplomat, smoothing over things. I do not speak as a politician to please people. What history will say about me is most important. I do not go after current popularity. Whether I become popular among the American people or not today is not important to me. I speak out as God dictates to me.

However, sometimes I do speak to the need of the people and at their level of perception, but there is nothing secret there. Jesus himself said, "I have yet many things to say to you, but you cannot bear them now." Sometimes I cannot speak certain things to the members or even to the leaders because they simply won't understand, not because I want to hide something from them. Each person's depth of understanding of the Principle is always different. St. Paul also said that sometimes he had to feed converts "milk" rather than "solid food" because they were not spiritually ready. Anyone must adjust to the level of understanding of his listeners. The Unification Church has no need for a clandestine operation.

Our past record is good proof. What have I done in the last thirty years, or what has the Unification Church done in Korea, Japan, or the U.S.? That is the proof. What we have done is to absolutely give ourselves to the service of others, the nation and humanity. Our primary job has been preaching the new truth and trying to win the peoples' hearts for God. Have you ever heard that we have tried to overthrow any government or rob a bank?

Sontag:

Oh, no, but a great deal of fear about you exists. People feel this way and the reasons are very difficult to get to.

Moon:

Probably this feeling comes from our enormous amount of energy and success. Here in America, people have never heard of any man from the Orient suddenly becoming such a prominent or controversial figure. Just a few years ago America had never heard of Reverend Moon, but now Reverend Moon pops up everywhere. They hear of a great deal of wealth, growth, and expansion. People cannot imagine what absolute dedication can bring in terms of achievement. So eventually they come to the conclusion that there must be some kind of conspiracy. Otherwise, how could these things be humanly possible? But I tell you, every achievement has been built by sweat, tears, and hard work. You are an eyewitness to the unprecedented dedication of our church. When people come to know God, many impossible things become possible. Each day is a miracle in our church.

Sontag:

One of the things that plagues the church now is the negative attitude developing in the country toward South Korea and President Park's government. Of course, it is true that there are ministers and leaders who have been jailed by him because of their protests. Are you aware of this, and what is your view on this?

Moon:

Many people suspect there must be a special tie between Park Chung Hee's government and the Unification Church. That assumption is absolutely untrue. Furthermore, the government has given our church no special privileges. As a matter of fact, for many decades I have been undergoing trials and ordeals because of the government's misunderstanding. The present government also initially gave a great deal of hardship to our church and is beginning to again. It is nonsense when people say there is a special tie between the Korean government and the Unification Church.

All we do is what our religious conscience dictates. We consider Communism the foe of mankind and the foe of God, so we take a strong posture in fighting against Communism, and we support a strong government against Communism. We do not support the North Korean takeover of South Korea. However, the government has not given any special privilege or consideration to us. There happens to be a common view on Communism between the Korean government and our religious conviction. I opposed Communism while in North Korea too. Because of my religious stand, the North Korean government put me in their worst prison camp for almost three years. Only God kept me alive.

During the *Newsweek International* interview I said that President Park does his job as the president of the country and I do my job as a religious leader. It is true, however, that many of the political prisoners in South Korea are pastors and religious leaders. The Korean government in the past never deliberately or directly opposed or oppressed religious freedom, whether Christian, Buddhist, or Confucian. However, the Korean government strongly reacts to any menace or threat to overthrow the government. This is where the problem came in.

The Unification Church has no intention of overthrowing or harrassing the government's position. We are aloof from

152

government policy. Still, there are many cases of government harrassment of Unification Church. It is very difficult to get our leaders out of Korea for world missions, and it is often difficult for our organizations in Korea to get certain permits, and so forth.

But as far as I am concerned, there is no direct religious persecution. If that existed in South Korea, I would immediately speak up against the Korean government. I will not tolerate that or gross violation of civil rights.

Sontag:

Of course, that's where the clouded issue comes. The religious men feel they're protesting for civil liberties.

Moon:

The amazing thing is the way they talk about civil rights. There are millions of civil rights being violated behind the Iron Curtain in the Soviet Union, Czechoslovakia, Hungary, Poland, et cetera, and the multimillions of civil rights being violated in China. Billions of people's civil rights are being grossly violated. Why do they not speak up against all these violations of civil rights? Why do they only try to magnify a few cases in Korea?

I do not condone any oppression of civil rights, but there should not be a dual standard. One principle and standard of righteousness should be applied to everybody, to every nation. Looking at this one standard, anybody who is truly concerned about human rights should inevitably become the absolute foe of Communism. Nothing in the history of mankind has violated more basic human rights than Communism. I am the foremost fighter for the preservation of human rights.

Therefore, we cannot condone a weakening of the South Korean government, thus making it vulnerable to North Korean invasion. The human rights of fifty million people are at stake. Any movement or campaign that works toward undermining the Korean government with its strong anti-Communist policy will inevitably invite the aggression of North Korea and the annihilation of the South Korean people. This would put 30 to 50 million people under Communist oppression in the name of "human rights." We should not become the naïve prey of Communism and turn over millions of innocent people to Communism.

It is a welcome relief that the Carter administration is speaking out strongly on human civil rights. I welcome that, but the Carter administration should develop one standard to apply all over the world. The same standards should apply to Korea and every other nation. Nowadays, because of the press, everything Korean is suffering. There is the exposé of Korean bribery and influence-buying and so forth. They even include President Park in a cloud of suspicion. I could never condone any illegal acts committed by the Korean government if there are any, but I have to ask why there is just accusation against Korea. Why isn't there anything against Soviet Russia and the KGB? Why should Korea, the most friendly nation to the U.S. and one nation which is desperately trying to survive, become a scapegoat? My genuine concern is that this double standard might push Korea into becoming another Vietnam. Then who will be next? The U.S. indeed is not far down the line.

I have never met President Park, and President Park has never had personal feelings toward me. There are absolutely no friendly ties between the two of us. Yet in principle I support a strong government and defense, and an absolute anti-Communist policy.

Sontag:

It is often said by religious critics of the church that the Principle does not stress the resurrection of Jesus as the central event for Christians and that this is the main issue in the charge of heresy against you. Would you comment on the significance of Jesus' resurrection?

Moon:

The Unification Church emphasizes the resurrection in a different light. The dispensation of God is a process of resurrection, so we look at resurrection as the process of restoration and salvation. We teach that the true resurrection of man is the resurrection of heart, the restoration of man's complete relationship to God. God is looking forward to the resurrection of all humanity. It is indeed his goal and the greatest event that will happen in all history. I emphasize the resurrection of the entire world, every individual and nation, as the ultimate fulfillment of salvation.

Resurrection is synonomous to *restoration*. So the Unification Church seeks physical as well as spiritual restoration. The kingdom of God on earth is really the resurrected world. In that world, there is the resurrection of the individual, where full spiritual perfection is achieved for eternity, then resurrection of the family, resurrection of the society, tribe, nation, and world. We become resurrected as sons and daughters of God; we become transformed into children of God.

It will be a glorious day when we all become resurrected and enter into his kingdom of heaven. Jesus was, is, and will be permanently the source of the resurrection of life.

154

Family portrait on the occasion of Kwon Jin Moon's second birthday, March 10, 1977, at Belvedere. The prepared table is a Korean custom. Front row, left to right: Heung Jin, Hyun Jin, Kook Jin. Back row, left to right: Hyo Jin, Sun Myung Moon, Mrs. Moon, Kwon Jin, Un Jin, In Jin, Sung Jin, Ye Jin.

Sontag:

I sense that life in the movement is changing in its form now, and it has changed at various points through its history. Do you see that there is change now coming to the life within the movement, in its structure, in its missions? Is there change going on and what future shape of the internal family is developing?

Moon:

I do not expect to see any major change in the make-up of our church, its structure, or the style of our life. I emphasize that our movement has always been centered upon families as the basic unit of heavenly society. The family emphasis is always the same. This means that more blessings in marriage will be given, more children will be born, more families will be created. Then we will become elevated from the present communal type of centers to family-oriented homes. The family will always be the basic unit of happiness and cornerstone of the kingdom of God on earth and thereafter in heaven.

Sontag:

But on the practical level, there might be more blessings, more marriage, more children, perhaps more individual family units, and everyone might not live in centers together as they do now. There might be some changes in

the life-style, such as phasing out the mobile fund-raising teams—you can't build a family while you're doing that!
Moon:
There will be a settlement. We don't have that now, but gradually we will be moving into family settlements. We will have our own enterprises and businesses. In the future we will have many, many places where families can be productive, raise their children, and build schools to educate the children. We'll get bigger. Our establishment will get bigger.

I have a plan to establish ideal cities and villages in many places. We will have productive, working communities where our members will support themselves economically. The atmosphere will be different from the outside world. Money will not be the central purpose, but while establishing productive businesses, our members will fulfill their responsibility to God and service to others.
Sontag:
One final question: I am an American and you are a Korean, and I think many people don't understand why you have come here. How do you see America?
Moon:
In light of the dispensation, the U.S. is the model Christian nation and therefore in the position of the second Israel. America's heritage is Christian. It should be the backbone of American strength. In the end, if America loses this heritage, it will lose its greatness and its true value. Backed by the Christian spirit, American democracy has survived and prospered. But if the Christian spirit is removed, America will become secular and barren. Divisons between gentile and Jew, black and white, rich and poor, will set in. Many potential crises will begin to erupt.

To make a long story short, God chose America as his final champion to serve as a builder of the kingdom of God on earth. That's America's role. But America's Christian spirit is its foundation, and unfortunately it is declining. A secular force has set in, and without some major spiritual change or reform, there will be no way America can fulfill her mission.

I came to America to fulfill several major missions. I came to revive the Christian spirit by igniting a new spiritual fervor with new spiritual truth. I came to start a Christian revolution in this country, which will bring back the heritage of this nation and will bring America back into a position to fulfill God's assigned mission.

Also I came to restore American families and American youth through a great moral principle. The degradation of the moral standard through drug problems, moral crises, and family problems is bringing American youth into a helpless position. Unless some new, effective youth movement comes, America's future is very dismal. This new spiritual revolution among American youth has been ignited.

I brought the Unification Church with me to America. Starting from this movement here in America, by influencing this great nation first, God can move the rest of the world. That is why I came to America.

I landed in Washington, D.C., on December 18, 1971. That's the day the active movement really began. Our members wondered how I could ever have dreamed of doing so much in such a short time. I cannot help but be astonished myself. But who did this? Not Reverend Moon; God did it. Only with the power of God could a stranger like me, not even knowing the English language, come into this country and accomplish the work I have done. Only with the power of God was it possible.

I have one hope. I am looking forward to the day that the American people will realize the true purpose of my coming to America. If America will realize why I came, what truth I am bringing, that will really be a day of hope in America. I did not come of my own will, and I did not bring my own message, but that of God. I came by his mandate and brought his words. Even though this movement started in Korea, Korea is not the central point; Japan is not going to be the central point. America is the central point for the entire success of the dispensation of God. Do you think that day will come?

Sontag:
People have been blind before and rejected leaders. What reason do you have to feel that America will respond?
Moon:
Even though the press and media are very important in terms of influence, in the long run the intellectual and academic communities, professors and students, are more important. Therefore, I put a great deal of emphasis in this area. We have started a student movement and a professors' movement, plus a new daily newspaper. Within a few years we need to gain the respect of American society, not because we want to be proud of ourselves but because we want to influence this people and nation in the direction of God. I am really committed to this.

My ultimate desire is to see this nation really come under God. Let it be one nation under God and cause the world to become one world under God. Because of ignorance and misunderstanding, America has mistreated me, but in my heart I have no hard feelings. I know why these situations develop, and I look at them as part of the plan of God. I came to make a declaration to America and to the world, and it needed to be spread quickly.

However, the thinking of the media is such that if no one had opposed me, they might have reported something like, "A religious man has come from Korea claiming to speak for God and he is trying to spread the message in America." It would have been only one small paragraph somewhere on page 78. But once a few people decided to oppose me and began to spread vicious rumors, the press was interested. Terrible story after terrible story of accusation came out. Now, whether positively or negatively, America knows me, and it happened quickly. At least I have America's attention. Now perhaps the people will be able to see the truth of God, the new revelation. The worst treatment America could give me is to ignore me, but she has not done that. Now I can show the truth.

My mission is a cosmic mission. My concern is for all of humanity, and not only this present world, but the world hereafter. My mission penetrates the past, present, and future, and encompasses all humanity.

Before I pass away, I must set the condition that the whole world, at one time or another, has had a chance to know, hear, and understand me. The message must be universally declared. This is the reason I myself must go all over the world and preach, and that is the same reason I sent out the Unification missionaries all over the world. This is heavenly strategy, but nobody understands it. Some think I am just a crazy man.

Many Unification Church members were prepared and destined to this calling. Others were just lucky; they happened to join and received great blessing. But they are all special. They responded to God's call and have volunteered to give themselves to the task of cosmic restoration. This extraordinary opportunity will occur only once in history, and it is unfolding here in America right now. This is an emergency for God and mankind.

Today America is a microcosm of the world. America's destiny will sway the destiny of the world and God's providence. He definitely has a central mission that he is working to unfold in this country. When I spoke at the rally in Yankee Stadium, I stated, "If there is illness in your home, do you not need a doctor from outside? If your home catches on fire, do you not need fire fighters from outside? God has sent me to America in the role of a doctor, in the role of a fire fighter."

On September 18, 1976, at the Washington Monument I also proclaimed, "God summoned me to this country to proclaim God's new revelation. And in particular, God called me to lead the young people of America, the leaders of tomorrow, back to God."

I have not heard any American religious leader making such bold statements. How then could a man from Korea speak like that? I am not speaking from my ego or seeking self-glory. I know who God is and what his mandate is. Every word I spoke was truly prophetic. Some people do not understand, yet I have to speak. I am a Korean, yet in the sight of God I am a true American, representing the core of the American spirit. If this spirit prevails in this land, America will live and prosper.

Suppose God suddenly appeared here in America. What would he say? Would he say, "You Americans are doing perfectly well. I am deeply delighted; keep on doing what you are doing"? The answer is no! Deep down in our innermost hearts, we all know that America is in spiritual, moral trouble, and if we continue the present trend, America will not be able to avoid the wrath of God. We know it.

When I speak as a messenger of God, I must speak the truth. Somebody must take up God's cause before it is too late. I came with a warning, a declaration to America. At the present time many people laugh at me. But history will never laugh at me, because I am not doing it. God is doing it. I am being used by God.

The spirit world is a labyrinth. That world is really a labyrinth. It is not humanly possible to find the proper path alone in the spirit world. You cannot find your destination unless you have a leader to guide you, unless someone paves the way. In that respect, Unification Church members are very, very fortunate people. Why? Our members have a spiritual light to lead the way, like a lantern before us.

What Can the Movement Teach Us?

Oh, can't you hear it, brother.
And won't you come along
To build the heavenly kingdom,
And sing a brand new song!

—from a Unification Church song

What Questions Does Moon Force Us to Answer?

In the first place, what is "life with father" really like? Ex-Moonies seem to vie with one another in magazine articles to see who can tell the greatest horror story about his or her treatment. Is there no truth to these lurid tales? There is, but how does one allow for exaggeration? Does no one have a successful and positive experience within the movement? Obviously thousands do and have. Reports often assert that Moonies have a glazed look. In observing Moonies in centers and at work, I have puzzled over this. "We do smile a lot," is one explanation the members give. They pray a lot too. Described from a different perspective, this can be reported as "how it should be." They are ecstatically caught up in a cause. If you believe in the cause, that's great. If you don't, the same phenomenon of intensity will appear "weird."

Sociologist John Lofland's *Doomsday Cult* (1966) is a thinly disguised account of life in the early Unification Church headquarters in the San Francisco Bay area. It offers, I would say from my exposure, some accurate observations about "Moonie" attitudes, techniques, and behavior. Two

160

questions about it loom large: (1) The book's final appraisal is that the movement is both struggling and unsuccessful. How, then, are we to account for its subsequent growth? (2) The author paints a rather negative picture of the life and the character of the people involved. All of them appear either a little pathetic or to be feared. Since many from that early missionary group have gone on to pioneer church growth around the world and are now successful leaders, what sources of energy have they found that Lofland did not see?

Rabbi Davis has described the atmosphere of Moon centers as a "boy-scout world," and in my experience it is a little like that. The problem again is that such a characterization can be taken in two ways. If you take it that "life" means to grapple constantly with a cast of characters from a TV mystery thriller, then Moon centers are escapes. On the other hand, if you think the point of religious communities is to create a life apart from and better than the world's, then the "warm, loving" atmosphere the Moon family tries to create is not an unrealistic sham but a testimony to their intention to inaugurate a new way of life. Take your choice.

Are there, then, no problems internal to a Moon center and the group of people who live there? Of course, all religious communities face problems when you have a group trying to live up to a strict ideal. As a visitor, I have undoubtedly seen the best of life in Moon centers. Underneath lie many problems, I'm sure. I lived one year in a Roman Catholic house in Rome. Problems of sex were constantly beneath the surface, and one monk said when I came upon a group in the hall, "Ah, you've arrived just in time to hear us bitch."

Not all whom I came to know that year in Rome are still in religious orders. Some surprisingly stayed and others surprisingly defected. Does this mean religious life as I saw it that year was a total sham? No, not in my mind. It does mean that religion is always "sticky business," because it often draws a troubled lot and then demands sacrifice from them. This is bound to produce explosions, some destructive. On balance, some are benefited and changed in desirable ways, and some are harmed.

When I visited a Unification center, the staff were usually prepared for my arrival. However, one thing which counterbalances the appearance of "staged performance" is that I also talked to those who report another and more negative experience. More important, I spent so many hours and days on these visits that, in the quiet spaces in between, I began to get some rather candid observations on life around me.

Perhaps the first thing to understand is that the Unification Church considers itself to be a "new Christianity." For members this means becoming the embodiment of a spiritual *plus* a physical ideal world. Establishing this dual kingdom was God's original intention, they say, but until now it has been possible only on a spiritual level. God has suffered, as the Moon movement has and must too, but their life aim is to restore God's joy—quite an animating spirit if it catches on. They believe the march of truth will now inevitably go forward, and it is one in which the members already participate today. They are living out the way to become true sons and daughters of God.

The descriptions in the press leave the reader with the impression that the church is something of a military organization. Like most charges, there is a grain of truth here, but it is not a very accurate impression. As I observed the operation of the church, the military image is misleading. Orders do not go out each day. The hierarchy is much less structured and fixed than that of a military organization or even the Catholic Church. The Moonies use the image of the family to describe themselves, and I think that is fairly accurate. You must, of course, have in mind the Oriental family structure and not the more mod and loose American family in which every member seems to be equal and going in his or her own direction, held together simply by a common roof.

In the Moonie family, elders have an authority of age and tradition, and church communication moves along family lines. You must go through channels, but these are the channels of family structure: older brother, uncle, cousin, patriarch. Contrary to a popular image, Reverend Moon does not issue daily detailed orders, at least as far as I can determine. Projects are adopted and leaders appointed, who then are on their own in pioneering the new development. Leaders' conferences are called frequently and family members travel constantly from all over the world to these gatherings. Plans are reviewed and frequent shifts take place, in addition to rapid transfers from one sphere of responsibility to another. Like the parable of the talents in the New Testament, each is left on his own with an assignment, but frequent accountings of his stewardship are called for.

People are ordered off to new assignments, particularly the younger members, but two factors need to be held in mind: (1) For those still in good standing, members express a willingness to do whatever they are asked to do for the cause. (2) When the leadership is sensitive, people are not blindly pushed about, but these shifts come with a certain amount of consultation and private negotiation. There is a flexibility of function and some option available, although shifts in campaigns come rapidly, and mobility is the movement's byword ("bring your sleeping bag"). Life is organized around the center leader, whose closest counterpart is the abbot of a monastic community now made co-ed. There are mistakes in the treatment of some individuals since the leaders often lack maturity.

The enterprises on which the Unification Church is engaged are probably much more numerous than even most church members are aware of. Leaving aside the whole spectrum of business and fund-raising operations, which are worldwide and as extensive as they are complicated; the cultural ventures, for example, symphony and dance, the sponsored lectures and meetings, et cetera, form an ever-changing kaleidoscope and vary from country to country. The average press account touches only the tip of the iceberg and tends to focus on a few oft-mentioned ventures like street fund-raising and real-estate purchase. One literally has to move around the world from center to center to get any idea of the breadth and variety of church activity and future plans.

One feature is the adaptability of members to new occupations. People with no experience are suddenly publishing a newspaper in London or New York or Tokyo. City boys find themselves farming north of London. Everyone finds himself or herself fund raising, either on the streets or through church-operated industries. Everyone witnesses in public and is pressed constantly to bring in converts. The core of recruiting is not sermon or ritual. Contrary to some impressions, life is built around a constant series of lectures. Everyone, therefore, who stays long in the movement finds himself acting in the role of a teacher. In strict contrast to Pentecostal techniques, which some imagine they use, the movement is quite academic in approach. The focus is on lecture and study, which may account for its strong appeal to intellectually oriented youth and to college-aged youth in general.

Training centers and training sessions form the core of the early experience. The *Divine Principle* is always the center of instruction, as it is in all the church's life, not Reverend Moon, as press accounts picture it. Instruction, training, and retraining constantly go on, but, underneath all this activity, what the outsider sees least is the formation of a living international family. Press attention centers on the mass marriage ceremonies. These carefully staged events involve a calculated number of persons who, on a selected date, receive the blessings of Reverend Moon and Mrs. Moon. Traveling among the centers, one is struck by the mixture of races, cultures, and countries patiently living in harmony. I have tried, but I cannot think of another new religious movement so genuinely international as the Unification Church. This is partly because almost all marriages are arranged, and each couple is matched by Reverend Moon.

The news stories make the public aware that this is a youth movement, but I do not think the full significance of that fact sinks in. In Korea, one witnesses a native church that now contains all age levels. Japan's membership is a

"The matching began in the largest lecture hall about 3:00 P.M. The men and women sat at the opposite ends of the room. Starting with the physically oldest members first and moving through various categories of age, position, etc., Master began to match the couples. When he would pick two people, they would go into a small adjoining room to consult with one another. If they accepted, they came out and bowed to Master, and everyone applauded. If they found some difficulty, they could try again or express a preference. Sometimes Master accepted their preference, sometimes he advised against it. Invariably, we found that Master's judgment was the best.

UC/NFP

UC/NFP

UC/NFP

UC/NFP

"Many of the couples hardly knew or had never even seen each other before. However, once they began to talk with one another after the engagement, after the blessing, in Tokyo and back in the United States visiting their parents, the real miracle became more and more apparent. . . .

"The most prevalent feeling was that God had been arranging the whole thing all along, that their mates had been created just for them. Master, knowing God's heart and will for each of them, had brought them together." *New Hope News,* March 10, 1975.

little older than the average age in the U.S., but the overlooked fact is that, in its day-to-day operations, the church is run by youth. It is a "Children's Crusade." Thus, untrained, college-aged kids are thrust into positions of responsibility and leadership for which they have little training. It is a maturing experience, as most will report. Still, serious mistakes are bound to be made—leading to more press horror stories.

When I went to the weekend training session at Boonville, we were told, "Our purpose in getting together is to experience brotherly love"—hardly an objectionable goal, since sex is taboo for unmarried Moonies. Our leader told us: "Maybe the things my heart wants are possible"— surely this goal has driven people to religion for centuries. "Joy fully, freely extended for the whole"—that is an attractive notion in an age dominated by selfish gratification. "We are to end conflict completely and unify on a common base," we were told. There is to be a revolution, a great change of heart, great love. "A mature person freely extends love and God is the source of love." The core of its attraction is the movement's underlying theme that basic changes, even perfection, in man and in society, which were not possible before, are so now—if we seize the day. Believing that draws every ounce of energy out of a person, whether it proves to be true in the long run or not.

In spite of all the time expended in investigation, reading, and interviews, I came to clear conclusions on relatively few issues. Each day further into the investigation convinced me that the movement raises every issue of importance in religion and contemporary society in an unavoidable way. But what are the remaining questions? Even to list them provokes rigorous self-examination.

1. Have many of our religious institutions drifted so badly that they no longer have clear beliefs and thus cannot attract the youth of today in a way that satisfies their religious desire?

2. Has our moral situation deteriorated into a destructive permissiveness, so that the attraction of Moonie straight life indicates our fall from anything like a pure life in religion?

Is there a new search for discipline and order among the young?

3. Has our family structure been ripped and torn, from inside and from without, so that it seldom offers the kind of warmth and guidance a child may need? What has the divorce rate done to this generation's children?

4. Have we talked of love but not known how to convey it in an unselfish way, except as gratification of our desires or as sexual passion?

5. How will the kingdom of God be brought to earth and how will God's will for man be realized if the religious proposals to date have not materialized?

6. Should a religion seek ascetic purity in a life of withdrawal from a corrupt or corrupting society, or must it plunge itself into the political, artistic, economic, and general cultural scene, in spite of conflict and possible tarnish?

7. Does God suffer grievously over man's state, so that we face a God of intense human passion who needs human effort to relieve his sadness and to restore joy to them both?

8. Is it possible to unite all religions, or does any such proposal simply become another divisive force greeted as such by the very allies it hopes to co-opt?

9. Is it the case that no one can receive truth directly but that each of us requires preparation, a demonstration of caring, the giving of love, and the right time before insight can be granted?

10. Does God continue revelation, so that his word is never final but unfolds with new times and places?

11. Do we require a central figure for religious conversion and growth, so that any attempt to pursue religion individually is doomed to failure? Does God require a family to be formed before religious life is possible?

12. Do we live in a messianic age, one different from others, in which God may act once again in decisive ways? Is it possible that the promised day for the completion of God's work is at hand, and how can we decide about the validity of signs that are claimed to foretell this?

13. Is it possible, or did God intend, for us to have a

theology that offers explicit answers to all the questions we ask? Is truth in some matters not really capable of final realization because basic differences of perspective and basic assumptions beyond the possibility of reconciliation are involved?

14. Do we require devils and saints to be personified, and can we expect greater claims to be made for leaders, pro and con, than circumstances warrant? Are our religious needs such that we first exaggerate our expectations from any religious figure and next exaggerate our disillusionment?

15. Does the establishment of the kingdom of God require human effort, so that God and man both suffer if we do not work to bring it into being?

16. Must the background of a man be pure if his later doctrine is to be believed, and can we expect slander as a matter of course whenever religious figures are involved?

17. If Jesus' disciples failed him, what kind of burden does that place on us, and what part of the kingdom of God depends on our loyalty and effort? If Jesus' mission is not complete, how and when will its completion come about?

18. Has Christian doctrine been so Western in its theoretical foundations that the time has come to try to join it with Eastern thought forms and cultural traditions?

19. Is it possible to do good things for the "wrong" theological reasons and nevertheless succeed in personal reformation when other, "purer" theologies fail?

20. When the Holy Spirit moves, does it always create pure doctrine, or can it genuinely inspire if not always through acceptable theological forms? Are all religions rough and crude in their origin so that they must go through a period of refinement of doctrine and practice before society can admit them?

21. How can we recognize a prophet of God at the time he is sent?

22. Is there a physical side to salvation which demands that we pay attention to physical restoration as well as spiritual?

23. In looking at the charges against the Unification

Church, how many could be made against other religious movements; are we really dealing with the question of secular vs. sacred goals?

24. Do all religions when they arise express humanity's hopes and offer more powerful promises than they can fulfill? Do they draw their energy from the power of the promise but finally become forced to accommodate to lesser goals?

25. What powers are present when we witness idealism, commitment, sacrifice, conversion, and youthful attraction?

The Birth of a New Religion

If we study the origin of the Unification Church and how it grew, we can learn much about how all religions develop in their first burst of disruptive growth. Quakers may be silent now, but George Fox disturbed churches and unleashed anger when he first started his movement against established religions. Wesley's conversion tactics were a public scandal. The Unification movement probably is not growing as fast as popular imagination suspects, nor as rapidly as its leaders hope, but its leap across oceans and its establishment itself demand an accounting.

We have open to us the chance to observe the birth of a new religion with all the classic characteristics: a leader, the formation of scripture, new revelations, rapid conversion, apocalyptic vision, and the call to repentance, as well as early repression and a hostile reaction to its growth and spread. We can also watch its transformation into an established world church from primitive origins in a remote spot.

As I began this project, the idea of an opportunity to observe how new religions are born had not entered my head. This was partly because I was at first tempted to treat the whole thing not very seriously and partly because I had little idea of either the church's origins or its doctrine. As I finally approached Korea and got closer to earlier and older members and heard their stories, it began to dawn on me that I was hearing a classical account of the birth, spread, and maturation of a new religion. One reason for my failure to sense this until quite late in my round of investigations was that I instinctively discounted the genuineness of the religion's origin and took for granted its status as a passing phenomenon, soon to disappear along with the flower children of previous years. From the press accounts, one gets the impression of a born-yesterday movement suddenly subject to a Madison Avenue hard sell.

In his book on Korea, *Victory Through Persecution*, Kurt Koch remarks: "It is strange to think that the city of Pyongyang had been the source of revival."* Christians who are now used to venerating Bethlehem as a holy place should stop and reflect that, in the Roman Empire, God's choice of Bethlehem in its day was thought indeed strange. I do not myself know whether God chose Pyongyang in North Korea as a point of entry into the twentieth century, but I do know that its reputation as the Jerusalem of the East has enough substance in it to make me stop and wonder at just what odd spot and in what unlikely form God might appear in our age. If we do not think Pyongyang is God's chosen city, where then might he choose to enter our life in this time?

The role of "heresy" in the birth of a new religion is also a fascinating question Moon raises for us again. That is, judged by most classical Christian theological positions, the *Divine Principle* does not conform to the norm. It offers new teachings about how God acts and how Jesus' mission is to be fulfilled. By this standard, of course, "liberal theology," process theology, Kierkegaard, Kazantzakis, and countless others are nonconformist, as are George Fox and Quakerism. Before we banish Sun Myung Moon, we have to ask, What role have such deviant theologies played in the past, and do new theologies have a significant role to play today?

Now that we have tamed and domesticated our once crude religions with scholarly patina and art forms, it disturbs and annoys us to be reminded of the socially

---

*Grand Rapids, Michigan: Kegal Publication, 1972, p. 25.

unacceptable quality of most of their origins. But what if the source of religion's vitality lies in its primitiveness? Then where should we look for religion today if we want it to move through the world like a fire to create new structures? Here, of course, we slam up against a long-standing division of opinion in outlooks on religion. Is religion's purpose to tame, domesticate, and shore up society's structures, as Marx and civil religion agree? Or, is religion born to burn like a fire, change lives, and alter the society it enters, as Moon and many liberals and evangelicals agree. All these religious perspectives differ about is the program and the means of change.

In the discussion following a lecture I gave at the Unification Seminary on some of my own views about God's nature, one of the questioners asserted that my account of God was "very strange." I replied with my favorite couplet: "How odd of God to choose the Jews" and chided him, "Any man who believes God chose a Korean who hardly speaks English to come to call America back to its religious mission as a nation should be careful about calling any view of God's nature 'strange.'" The *Divine Principle* does give a strange version of God's action, but the issue is: Is God's action sometimes odd to our eyes, and what alternative vision can we have of how and where he acts today?

If we are seeing a new religion in the pangs of its birth, what is to be done about it? The first thing that needs to be done is to find out what God is like and how he can be made real to others. We live in a day of some confusion over this matter, when to many people God seems distant or inactive. For a Moonie this is not so. Consequently, he knows exactly what must be done about his experience of God's suffering and love: He must work to relieve the divine suffering by recreating the kingdom of heaven on earth and also pass along that love to others through self-sacrifice. One of the most frequent comments made in the interviews was that "God has been made real to me." These reports must be explained, no matter how negative one's personal appraisal of Reverend Moon and the

173

movement might be. It is, in fact, difficult to explain the convert's vivid experience of God if we accept only the dark side of the movement.

Such a vision of God puts a heavy burden on the believer, for now it is literally his responsibility if God's mission fails. It is a fearful load to carry, but it does help explain the pressure each Moonie feels concerning the importance of contributing maximum effort. God not only demands it; God needs it and cannot do without it. Seeing God in this way raises the important question: What can God do and what must humans do? Moon does not lack a doctrine of grace, but he wants to stress that God grants man pardon, shows him a way, but then man must accomplish his part while also carrying others along.

This new religion causes us to ask: Does God need a nation as well as individual loyal followers? The will of God, the Principle teaches, was that his son prosper on earth. Jesus came to erect a kingdom of heaven on earth, not to die. The death of the son shattered the heart of God, so that Sun Myung Moon has come to speak of the suffering of God. But the revealer of truth traditionally draws persecution, whereas what is needed is a nation rising up as God's new instrument of reform. We have the spiritual foundation for the kingdom laid by Jesus' life and work, but now a people and a nation are needed to work on a worldwide scale for physical restoration.

Symbolically speaking, Jesus should have reformed Jerusalem and then moved on to challenge Rome. Only a confrontation with the major powers could have released the world of his time to reformation. But Jesus could not complete such a mission himself. His followers had already deserted him before the first political level was reached, leaving him without power as he faced Pilate. This brings us to the movement's central notions of indemnity and restoration. Before we can complete Jesus' unfulfilled mission, we must pay indemnity through struggle and suffering. For those so purged, money and power can now be used for good where others use it selfishly. One must use

174

earthly advantages if one is to succeed on the physical level of restoration.

Can the heavenly kingdom come to earth by adopting material power? This new religion claims that is what must be done; its involvement in political and economic power offends those who claim religious life should be purely spiritual and detached. Consequently, Moonies are little understood and even less accepted. Like the Marxists, the Moonies also admit the necessity of wielding power. For the Marxist, it is absolutely clear where power lies (controlling the means of production), and he will do anything to gain control for "good ends," even if his motives look impure in the midst of the power struggle. Marxism promises a utopia on earth as the result of capturing power. Must religion abandon the stage without offering a counterrevolution in politics? Moon does not think so.

The goal of every true Moonie is not small: to build a world that reflects the divine ideal. Jesus suffers (and God too) because the people fail to respond. If this is the case, each follower knows the burden is on him not to fail the offered opportunity. Three kings, it is reported, came to bring Jesus gifts at his birth, but they did not know the Principle. Jesus needed the kings to take care of him and educate him, Moonies say. The kings' early homage was not enough, and with the crucifixion it came to an empty gesture. If John the Baptist had bound together with Jesus, it would have given him tremendous credibility, Moon doctrine reports. The disloyalty of others (that ancient sin) caused Jesus' mission to remain incomplete, so that loyalty becomes the chief virtue in this age, overpowering all other ethical concerns.

As we watch Moon's one-time followers turn on him and seek to destroy the church they formerly worked so hard for, we understand the transition Jesus experienced from Palm Sunday to Good Friday. Those who proclaim a man to be a messiah are likely, we learn from reading scripture, to turn on the man they once celebrated and seek to crucify him. We, and they, expect too much immediately from our

175

religious leaders. When the pain and work required to produce profound change in our lives becomes evident to us, we tend to withdraw our support. The Moon movement today is moving from Palm Sunday celebration toward Good Friday desertion. As long as Moon lives and the Unification Church exists, it serves as a reminder to every former member of his or her hope for the religious transformation once longed for and believed possible.

As we listen to the stories of those who leave the Unification Church, the question is, Are we hearing anything different from the disillusionment of so many who join a movement with high expectations only to find the life within either more prosaic than or perhaps even at odds with the official, ideal doctrine. Few religions deliver immediately either what they claim or what we expect. Most movements are plagued with workers who lead less than exemplary lives or go too far in their zeal for the cause. Certainly the Moon movement is not free of error and excess; the stories of that are too many to discount. But, is it in fact worse or better than any religious institution that cannot live up to a standard set higher than men and women can reach?

The Charges That Inflame Us

Because the charges most often made against the church tread on every sensitive area in society today, they have a tendency, merely upon mention, to inflame the hearer. There is no chance to debate the issue; the mere statement of a charge is sufficient to convict. Emotion concludes the matter, while reason need not bother about it. No solution I uncovered lies on the surface; rather, each requires some consideration in depth. What are the charges?

1. *The Unification Church separates children from their families, creating an alienation of natural affection, particularly with the doctrine of True Parents.* This is the single most inflammatory issue for the press. The stories of parental anguish spur the anti-Moon movement. A multitude of factors are involved:

a. The pattern of family disruption has been universal as the church has expanded in each country, although perhaps it varies in severity. It is also true that most new religious movements create the same disruption at their beginning, and it is a phenomenon predicted for an eschatological time.

b. Family disruption tends to subside after the initial missionizing thrust and as the church becomes established as a known part of life.

c. The doctrine of True Parents is hard to explain because it is both central to the movement and much misunderstood popularly. Due to the Fall, all human beings live under original sin and thus no one now lives an ideal life. The Unification doctrine of the plan for restoration calls for beginning a pure line in which families can give and take love without disharmony. The True Parent is the founder of this new line, although that involves no rejection of biological parenthood. It should create a wider sphere of loyalty and affection, but it does turn the convert away from his own family centeredness to a world-family ideal.

d. Perhaps the greatest irony of the movement is that it announces itself as bringing peace, love, and unity but begins by arousing hostility and creating family alienation. One could claim that they preach one thing and act out its opposite, but that does not explain the puzzle adequately. First, there is the long-range vs. the short-range goal. The disciple is at first torn away from his family, but the long-range goal is to unite. This program is long, carefully worked out, and involves many prior conditions. Thus, in the short run the family and other comforts must be sacrificed. Of course, if you do not believe in the program or the goal, you see only the immediate disruption.

e. Have children actually been held from their parents and contact denied? Undoubtedly this is true in some cases. Church officials go further and admit many mistakes in handling family relations. However, the interesting and sad fact is that it is sometimes the convert who wants to avoid family contact. This happens for a wide variety of reasons, and then the child uses the church as an excuse or buffer when parents turn hostile. The unfortunate tendency is for the child to draw away from his or her family just when coming together is what is needed. Perhaps the greatest subtlety in the problem is brought out if we ask, Did the church cause the family breach or simply bring into public view what had been a private fact? One member claims that if your family relations were close before, they can remain close after. But if they were bad before, the abrupt change brings every problem unavoidably to a head. This may be true to some extent but probably is too simple an answer.

In their interviews, many members said that their parents thought they were close or understood them, but it was not true. Often the new member reports involvement in a restless search before meeting the Unification Church. Family and friends did not know about this because, until the point of conversion, it was an inner search and a private alienation. If difficulties and a lack of communication exist, as long as the child stays on an accepted societal track, alienation can be accepted. But if the child claims he has solved his problems and is happy in the church, most parents have trouble accepting this because the new goals and life-style are so foreign. We have grown used to accepting certain external forms as a sign of happiness. When these are absent or altered, it is hard to recognize happiness because it comes in strange dress.

f. Parents report that they cannot talk to their children and are startled by the change in demeanor. After intensive training, the child has a new world view and mission. According to doctrine, it cannot be blurted out abruptly. If the convert meets hostility or unbelief, it drives him to silence, a phenomenon familiar to all parents in dealing with children around the ages of eighteen to twenty-five. Since the child possesses a "truth," he becomes the teacher and feels in a way privileged, or perhaps superior, as a result of what he has now learned. This creates a reversal of roles that is difficult for the parent to accept. It is often exaggerated by the young who have so long been held in the role of the one needing instruction.

g. Because of their belief in the existence of a spirit world with good and evil forces, new members may see their negative parents as under the sway of Satan. This creates a barrier, even when the ultimate aim is to overcome the opposition with love. The church may advise the convert to separate from his parents until a "more propitious time" arrives. As a Westerner who believes in open confrontation, I find this indirect technique hard to accept. Yet the new member bides his time until the conditions are "right" for parental contact. Belief in a spirit world can be exaggerated and overdone, but it is also true that confronting hostility directly in an emotionally charged setting does not lead to more understanding unless careful preparation is made.

h. In the rash of angry-parent stories, we overlook the fact that not all parents are hostile and not all members have bad relations with their parents. Some parents are positive, supportive, and even appreciative. The difficult ones tend to get the headlines since their stories are much more interesting. Numbers are hard to estimate, but perhaps the largest share of parents are silent and reluctantly accepting. If all parents were hostile and no member communicated with his or her family, this would be an easy problem to solve. But we face a spectrum of reactions, all the way from hostile to skeptical to openly accepting. Of course, in some cases (particularly in the Orient), whole families may join, or children may draw their parents into membership.

2. *The Unification Church severely damages the convert's personality and often is the source of long-term psychological problems.*

a. All religions attract people in trouble, many with severe emotional difficulties. The question is not whether some are lost but whether the cure rate is sufficient to justify the difficulties involved. Numbers are hard to pin down. Some psychiatrists report having seen thirty to fifty patients. Those touched by the movement number in thousands. The real question is, Did the experience in the movement, its training methods and its life-style, of itself cause or induce the psychological difficulty, or did the experience simply expose it?

b. From members' testimony we know that many assert they have been helped and changed in beneficial ways. We must note that it is the parents, slightly more than their children, who claim that harm is done by the church. This often means that the person in question has changed dramatically, which leaves open the question of whether the alteration is for good or for ill. Unless one rejects totally the phenomenon of religious conversion, we are at best dealing with a mixed result. This leads to the conclusion that the harm or benefit depends on the individual situation and cannot be generalized. Of course, such a conclusion will not hold for those who reject the movement's doctrine and on that basis alone deny that it can produce any good. But this turns the issue into a theological, not a psychological, one.

c. One confusing factor is the introduction of forcible "deprogramming" techniques. These have been reported earlier along with kidnapping. The point to note is that in the case of those deprogrammed, it is hard to tell which psychological symptoms are the result of the shock technique necessary to extract the child and which are directly the result of the movement's training methods. Psychiatrists say that a year's recovery period is usually needed before the person is "normal" again. But how much of the disorientation is due to the forced detachment of the person from the idealistic cause and the Unification "family" support? The forces that lead to human deterioration are hard to isolate.

d. One psychiatric social worker commented that the devoted member's idealistic exaggeration of life in the church family is matched by the overly negative exaggeration of the ex-member once he or she is deconverted. When the glamour of devotion to an ideal is gone for the ex-member, then his personal importance depends on swapping horror stories. What once was devotion to a cause becomes a crusade against the cause. Both require total absorption of the individual and encourage the human tendency to exaggerate.

e. Can we explain some, but not all, of the problems that

the press reports (e.g., families denied access to children) as a discrepancy between theory and practice? I have indicated how the theory legitimizes many practices that outsiders question, e.g., fund raising and Moon's life-style. In this case, the practices do not represent a violation of professed ideals but rather are the embodiment of a goal. Yet, in other cases which are the source of general anguish, leaders deny that these practices reflect their intentions, such as separation of child and family. Just as Marxism has often been most objectionable not in theory but in practice, so the Moon hierarchy will have to "clean up its own house" if it is not to allow aberrant practices to make its professed ideals appear a sham.

3. *The training and conversion techniques amount to brainwashing or mind control and rob the individual of his free will, so that any supposed voluntary acceptance is somehow false.*

a. This charge is perhaps the most difficult to deal with adequately. Let us note first that no member interviewed accepted anything like the brainwashing charge and most laughed at it. One cannot judge all members, but some certainly engage in intelligent and natural discussion and seem well in charge of their faculties. The first thing to say is that the term *brainwashing* is probably misleading, and the discussion of the issue would be enhanced if the term were omitted. Its use indicates that offensive and violent tactics were employed, and I discovered no hint of a prison mentality in any training center.

b. Pressure *is* applied. Of that there is no question. Is it so severe and subtle and hidden that it robs a person of his "free will"? Let us bypass the question of free will and note that persuasive techniques are a fact of life and one had best learn to deal with them rather than think there is some safe place where no one applies any pressure to gain support. Given this situation, the training sessions of the Moonies have some distinctive features, but essentially, they seem to be little different from the "mountain camp" retreat settings that have been the stock-in-trade of quite acceptable religions for centuries. Is it the religion then, more than the technique, that really is being questioned?

181

c. If the charge of mind control comes from ex-members, we have to ask how much of it is self-justification to explain away their once ardent commitment to a cause they now reject? If it comes from parents, how much of the charge is made to cover the hurt of facing the fact that Johnny might have voluntarily turned away from his inherited life-style and opted for something different?

d. "Free will" has baffled philosophers for years. We cannot settle the issue, but we should be careful of any assumed definition that is regarded as the unquestionable explanation. If free will is taken to mean lack of commitment, if it disapproves most of all of total commitment, and if it requires a cautious suspension of judgment, then by this definition most religious conversions will fail the test. We should be careful of assuming without question that the world is such that, rationally, it never permits a total commitment. That assumption rests on a particular metaphysical view of the basic uncertainty in the world, and it is not an obvious fact about all experience. If free will means an absence of all persuasive influences, some laboratory experiments might meet this criterion, but most important life issues are decided in the "heat of the kitchen," to borrow Harry Truman's phrase.

One psychiatrist defined free will as "a capacity to take in data, sort out and compare, deal with ambiguities, come to a conclusion to act without referring to a source of truth. Behavior should be occasionally idiosyncratic and should deal with ambiguities, recognize that they are there and act without needing to be certain." As is obvious, such a definition involves a nest of assumptions. Almost any Moonie could accept these criteria, except perhaps "without referring to a source of truth," "occasionally idiosyncratic," and "act without needing to be certain." In some cases, new-member behavior might even fit these, but more in practical matters than in doctrine. Individualism, a lack of any truth, and the impossibility of certainty should not be assumed as desirable when in fact these involve great questions. Some quite rational men and women still think certainty is possible.

e. A psychiatrist who is knowledgeable on brainwashing techniques said that the church clearly uses some aspects of the classical techniques, such as control of the environment, but it does not employ the whole set of conditions that constitute mind control. Every movement that is out to change people employs some instruments to control thought, e.g., the narrowing of perspective. These become pernicious only at some critical point when the mind is coerced beyond possible self-control. One issue is whether totalism ever produces a good result. It can, but of course it also has the potential of becoming destructive. When asked about deprogramming by way of contrast, the psychiatrist replied, "I'm opposed to coercion of the mind in any form"—which I think summarizes the matter succinctly.

f. Are abnormal conversion techniques used, even if *brainwashing* is a misleading term? Constant attention and affection is paid to the guest, and members cite this display of love as one of the attractions that pulled them in. The doctrine is progressively revealed ("deception" is a separate issue). The novice is urged to consider and explore further. The individual, chances are, is in a transitional phase, but that applies to most in this age bracket and to almost all who explore religious solutions. Is withdrawal made difficult? Like the peer pressure on any college campus to try marijuana and sex, many young people find the invitations flattering. Yet, of the thousands who attend training sessions, only a handful eventually join. Such a low conversion rate would disappoint most professional recruiters. Once having joined, however, the peer pressure to stay in the movement probably makes it more difficult for the convert to decide to get out than it was to decide to join.

4. *Sun Myung Moon has esoteric and exoteric teachings. He preaches love and unity publicly, but privately he urges questionable techniques and more ego-centered goals.*

a. Does Reverend Moon teach anything different in private to his followers than he admits in his public proclamations? I asked this question of members around the world and got every answer but yes. You can say I ought not to trust their answers; they were given to an outsider, to one uninitiated into the mysteries. Still, in reading mountains of material, although I did learn many subtleties about the necessity for "slow revelation," I can only report that I never uncovered or stumbled across anything like private teachings in blatant contradiction to public doctrines.

b. What I did learn is that their doctrine of the active spiritual world that invades human life makes them feel that everyone needs careful preparation before he or she is capable of hearing and absorbing the full truth. Slow induction and right circumstances are both important, and one cannot expect a novice to understand on the same level as the seasoned member. Trial and suffering and the paying of indemnity are necessary foundations too, so that finding the truth is not an easy matter but a long trail. Most people outside the church miss the fact that those inside are under constant pressure to continue to "grow spiritually." Thus, there is no single level of truth but rather progressive revelation. It is hard to reveal the truth of the inner life to someone outside who has not himself gone through these spiritually maturing experiences.

c. It is the series of talks by Reverend Moon called *Master Speaks* that most people have in mind when they report on "hidden teachings" of an explosive nature. The contents of *Master Speaks* have already been reviewed, but it should be noted that these are "family conversations," and we might expect them to be somewhat different. The question is whether contradictions are involved. Reverend Moon is speaking to his followers, in Sunday service or on special occasions, and the enthusiasm generated by this situation might leave the words open to misunderstanding. At the least we must admit that we are dealing with doctrine open to a variety of interpretations and also one that is easily slanted.

d. But are the private claims stronger and more blatant than the printed *Divine Principle?* For now, I can say that there does seem to be a rising sense of urgency as the timetable comes closer to its predicted date of completion. The growth and success of the movement do seem to generate a kind of euphoria and exhilaration and pressure. Most of the time, however, the pronouncements are quite consistent with the *Divine Principle*. The suspicion of secret teachings stems more from either a failure to understand the public doctrine (and understanding it is no easy task) or a total rejection of it. This takes the form of suspecting sinister hidden teachings.

5. *Mobile fund-raising teams use fraudulent means to collect donations and purposefully conceal their relation to Reverend Moon and the movement.*

a. This is a difficult charge which, in my estimation, does not allow a single answer. On the one hand, enough instances have been reported to make it certain that deception sometimes occurs. On the other hand, the sales technique clearly is to establish a personal relationship first and not to hit the people they approach with the church name immediately. Some teams operate legally and do identify their connection when questioned. It is clear that top-level official church advice is for honesty and legality. If you insist on immediate labeling, their fund-raising techniques will always seem "dishonest," no matter how legally it is done.

b. Given the furor in America over fund raising, two factors are overlooked: (1) In other countries, where public fund raising is prohibited, the church earns its money in other ways. The openness of America to direct charitable appeal is unique on the international scene. (2) As the church becomes more established, its money raising will assume more orthodox forms, for example, industries, newspapers, services, fishing, et cetera. We can already observe a shift to more conventional enterprises in America. The great fund-raising effort on the streets was an emergency measure undertaken to establish the movement in America and to fund its elaborate public programs. Whatever one thinks of these objectives, one has to admit their amazing success. They came from nowhere and they did it.

c. "Heavenly deception" is the controversial term that many object to, and it is slippery to pin down. That is, for the purpose of a good cause, is it acceptable to lure your subject by half-truths or statements that deceive because your intention is not and cannot be understood by the "subject"? In my experience, members joke about "heavenly deception" among themselves, but when pressed, this seems to mean something like "effective public relations" or "good sales techniques." When you ask if open, conscious deception is approved, that is denied. However, they admit that zealous members overstep the bounds of propriety in their eagerness to succeed and to keep up their fund-raising quotas. The issue is whether these are individual slips or a practiced technique of the church.

The programs of the Unification Church do not fit the standard church-charity stereotype. I suspect it is the use of the funds collected that bothers most people, not so much any real knowledge of illegal or fraudulent means. The detractors are sure fund raising is largely deceptive; the church members treat it as work with a high spiritual aim. Money goes into centers, real estate, and academic conferences. This is a far cry from the relief of economically deprived people which most churches espouse as their mission. The Unification movement, I think, believes their "public influence" programs are the way to bring the kingdom of God on earth. Few outside accept this program and so cannot accept the fund raising as legitimate either.

d. If deception is practiced in fund raising—and there is some—still it is surprising to learn the attitude of the practicing member toward what we take as an unpleasant task. The ex-members are disgruntled, of course, but many active members speak of their fund-raising days with a nostalgia that surprises the outsider. Why? The answer is connected with the strong "pioneering spirit" in the church and also with their belief in the necessity to suffer and struggle in order to lay the foundation for spiritual success. Some members may have had bad experiences with their teams and leaders. Others speak of it as a time of closeness, struggle, and a way of carrying their witness out into the streets. Fund raising has for them a spiritual dimension, which few outside can see.

6. *The church forms and uses a constantly shifting series of front organizations to disguise its activities and to lure support under false labels.*

a. One thing is obvious to anyone who follows the history, growth, and international scale of the movement: They are into 1001 activities. Shifts in projects come with a rapidity members joke about and find hard to keep pace with themselves. Antichurch groups have compiled lists of organizational titles, and probably they have found only half of them. More humorously, the odds are that no one in the church hierarchy could give you a complete list of activities the church has had going in every country in its history. They move too fast to keep long records and are too interested in today's new ventures.

The church does use 1001 organizational names, but is it either accurate or helpful in understanding church procedure to call them "front" organizations? The issue is not whether the church sponsors a multitude of organizations but whether it is "upfront" and open about its connection to each group. Is the Pilgrim Fellowship at my Congregational Church a front organization? No, my own church sponsors it as a special activity for youth. Is the Unification Church equally open about the various activities it sponsors?

b. First of all, we have to note the human failing of not noticing very carefully the sponsorship of many activities we join. As has been said, many people really don't read their mail. Only later when some question arises do we inquire, but then whose fault is this? In my travels, I crossed paths with more church activities specially named than I cared to keep track of. But with the sole exception of the special case in San Francisco, the connection to the church never seemed consciously hidden. On the contrary, leaders all over the world were excited and proud to outline the hundreds of forms that their activity took in that locality or country. The doctrine prescribes that energy must be poured out on many fronts simultaneously.

c. What is the exception? The Creative Community Projects Foundation in San Francisco/Berkeley was founded primarily by church members, but they prefer to maintain the image that it is not a direct church operation. And most stories of church deception center around this special Bay Area operation. Leaders explain this by saying that Berkeley of the sixties would not respond to any organized church, and they wanted to be free to involve nonmembers in their projects without commitment. Whether this justifies the situation or not, I think the lack of clear church identification is a mistake even in this case, and it is also the origin of much generalized allegation. But if sponsorship is designated, then *front organization* is not a helpful term. That should be reserved for clandestine, secret operation—a situation that does not describe the total Moon movement's activity accurately.

7. *The church raises great amounts of money which go illicitly to support the leaders' ostentatious style of living.*

a. Initially, we must note that the church and Reverend Moon lived in poverty for years, so that we are dealing with a new phenomenon when we observe the movement's present opulence. The other fact difficult for outsiders to understand is that the movement never intended to live constantly in poverty. In fact, the doctrine predicts material success and specifically aims for it on religious grounds. We have, of course, been agonizing for a long time over the question of whether we should require vows of poverty from all full-time religious people. Some individuals adopt this style, but there has been no universal agreement about the virtue of poverty among all who are religious. Many religions control great resources.

b. As we deal with the problem of wealth and its use, we face a most interesting—and controversial—aspect of Unification doctrine. The financial world is to be "restored" too, they say. The way to do this is to plunge into the middle, to secure financial power, to gain financial allies, and to demonstrate in practice the ideal that material means can and must be bent to the service of God's work. This is the only way the Kingdom can come on earth. If we view this as a counterpart of Marxist goals, it offers a capitalist alternative. The means of production must be controlled for the benefit of all, but the proposal is to do this through capitalist economics now bound to Christian ideals.

To one of a socialist or political left leaning, this of course does not seem to be the way to go. In fact, it is contrary to any religious view that combines Christianity and a Marxist social program. All one can do is to note the issue at stake and also recognize that Moon is not alone in this alliance of economics and religion, even though it is out of fashion in some church circles. Many cannot even consider this as an acceptable alternative religious program, so feelings do run high. The use of wealth by established churches is, was, and will remain a prime religious issue.

c. The basic underlying dilemma is whether any one individual or any group of the leadership profits personally from the accumulated wealth. Of course, the leaders enjoy certain privileges of control, as any executive does. This is not only acceptable to them but is sought for as part of their religious program. They categorically deny that anyone, Moon included, uses these resources for his personal gain. If any diverting of funds to personal control should come to light, this would not only be questionable but false to the doctrine. Active members express their approval and trust of the way the hierarchy exercises its stewardship. One knowledgeable secular editor expressed his doubts on the matter, even though he did not question the sincerity of the religious intention. It remains a difficult issue, and it is not apt to go away.

d. Does the movement have a sufficient emphasis on helping the poor, the downcast, the neglected of the world? In this instance, the evangelical stress on missions, on securing converts, and on the salvation of souls is the best model for our understanding. We live in an age of extreme consciousness about social programs, and we often stress outreach programs to the neglect of winning souls and the care of our spiritual life. Nevertheless, the Moon movement probably overemphasizes the need to win support from intellectuals and prominent leaders, which leads them to spend a disproportionate amount of time and money on schemes of influence. Of course, their doctrine links winning this support with the way of salvation. However, if their day of restoration is postponed, perhaps their attention will turn to ministering to souls in need on a nonprestige basis rather than service in return for potential influence.

8. *The church invests vast sums in industry and in real estate and is building a financial empire, not a church.*

a. This, of course, is a continuation of the issue posed in charge number 7. The movement is buying prominent pieces of real estate, and they do control various industries around the world. For them, this is not a denial of their religious goal. It is a confirmation of the truth of their revelation beyond the wildest dreams of the early poverty-stricken Korean disciples. Since the aim of restoration includes physical and economic restoration, they take great pride in the way they purchase, renovate, improve, and use our decaying physical monuments, for example, the New Yorker Hotel.

From its origin, as I learned in Korea, the church has engaged in various business enterprises as a church family. They were not terribly successful in the early years, but their entry into the commercial field was an original announced goal. The success and expansion of the Japanese church really triggered the Korean development and bankrolled the missionary movement abroad. Just as the pattern of members' living in centers as a family group developed in Japan and spread, so Japanese economic success set a pace for the rest of the church's development. It aims to control vast sums, but to do so in order to fulfill God's will and thus establish the physical Kingdom on earth. The aim is unselfish. The issue is whether it can be carried out without corrupting its ideals by its very success.

b. What about the way the movement uses the money that the members collect and the industries produce? Their doctrine makes plain why they expend effort on congressional and U.N. relations and why they spend large sums on academic conferences. They are free to do so if they want, and I find little but enthusiasm for these projects among the members. Other churches spend money on physical plants, music, et cetera, which bear little relationship to the relief of human suffering either, and few object to that. Personally, however, I do not think the restoration of mankind will come through influencing academicians or politicians. I do not share Moon's hope for these social avenues of reform. On the other hand, I see nothing sinister in the motivation, only a lack of understanding that intellectuals often tend to undercut the roots of religious practice and life.

9. *The movement is unchristian and anti-Semitic, spreading hatred and division, not unity and love.*

a. The Unification Church does us the favor of raising once again the question of what it means to be "Christian" and who has a right to claim the title. We should begin by admitting that, although many standards are offered and some are more or less widely accepted, all who call themselves Christian still have no universal agreement on a creed. We have no single authoritative, established church in America. Over the centuries, we have witnessed many proposals to settle this argument definitively, but we are no nearer to a final answer than we ever have been. In fact, I suspect that final agreement about Christianity is, in the nature of the case, impossible. Perhaps uniformity is not even desirable, given our record of using dogmatic formula as an excuse to bludgeon those whom we oppose.

The situation we face is this: (1) The judgment one makes depends on the standard set for "Christianity." Moonies are Christian according to some definitions and not according to others. But most important and also most complicating, (2) they claim Christianity for themselves and so cannot be dismissed without a hearing. Given the record of the various councils we have called to settle these doctrinal matters, we should not be too optimistic about a final settlement of this question. However, raising the question of who is a Christian ought to shock us into new awareness. Challenges to orthodoxy from outside should startle us into reexamining the adequacy of our own responses to the question, Who is Jesus? The Moonies have a clear answer; do we? Individually, maybe yes. Organizationally, probably no.

Without recounting the doctrine in detail, the interpretation given in the *Divine Principle* of Jesus' role is obviously not the orthodox one. However, it does not lie at some opposite extreme but actually is very close to tradition on many major points. The real difference lies in the question of the Second Coming and how the final Kingdom is to be established. Quoting New Testament solutions on this matter misses the major point: The Moonies claim new revelation in the *Divine Principle*, which provides a key to clear up previously misunderstood biblical questions—a not too unusual claim of new groups. If you accept this new revelation as being "of Christ," they are fellow Christians. If you do not, you are left with doctrinal differences as old as New Testament days.

b. The charge of anti-Semitism is actually more difficult to pin down. Movement officials deny the charge, so at least there is no acknowledged anti-Semitism. But who is anti-Semitic? This question should perhaps be left open with the ironic note that it is not likely all Jews will agree on one definition either. However, the movement draws an unusually large percentage of Jewish converts who obviously don't see it as anti-Semitic. Why does it attract such a high percentage of Jews, many of whom occupy leadership roles? That is an unanswered question in my own mind, and it adds a subtle complexity to the hostile charges from official Jewish sources. The Moonies are a new messianic movement like many in the history of Judaism which have arisen during particularly troubled times.

10. *Moon is blasphemous in claiming to be the new messiah now on earth to usher in a new age, usurping a role reserved for Jesus.*

a. Few outsiders accept the subtlety of the question involved or have the patience to try to unravel it. To my knowledge, there is nowhere recorded the blatant claim by Reverend Moon, "I am the messiah." His followers vary in their assertions, although those who make strong claims for him have grounds to do so. The *Divine Principle* certainly "reveals" that the time is again right for God to try to establish his Kingdom on earth, that the Lord of the Second Advent will come from the East and probably from Korea, that Reverend Moon has been called to announce this and to play a central role.

b. We also face the complication of the messianic secret. That is, perhaps the followers know and believe Moon to be the expected Lord of the Second Advent, but they do not disclose this to outsiders because the time is not right nor are the people prepared. This would be a simple answer if it were not for the complexity of the Principle's assertion that even this new attempt will not necessarily succeed. God is man- and nation-dependent, so the attempt could fail again. Jesus carried the mission part way (which is an orthodox point), and he succeeded spiritually more than any man before him. But the final resolution is not entirely in God's hands (theologically, this is the most debatable point in their doctrine). No success is predictable in advance, but they are again calling on us to make the effort. The time is propitious for us to succeed in establishing the earthly Kingdom with the aid of the spirit world.

c. Since his followers do vary in their own private response to the question, Who is Sun Myung Moon to you? we know that no dogmatic formula is enjoined as the price of membership. The effort to establish God's kingdom on earth takes precedence, and there is no question about Moon's leadership in that campaign. Success depends on the loyalty of the followers. Moon cannot fulfill the messiah's role by himself. Jesus was not able to carry his mission to full fruition, not through his own fault but as a result of the failure of those around him. The realization of that fact accounts for the intensity of discipleship in Moon's movement, but it also implies that Moon could fail in his leadership. Nothing is guaranteed to him except a call to the attempt at this time.

d. Of all traditional Christian doctrines, the Second Coming of Jesus is today the least sharply defined in most Christian minds. Probably this is rightfully so, and some even dismiss expectation of the event as nonessential. How do we, then, expect God's kingdom to be fulfilled, if we agree that the record of established Christian institutions to date leaves the question in doubt as to whether we have progressed toward the Kingdom since Jesus' time? That is, given the destructive and evil forces loose in the world, are they any more in God's control now than earlier? And how will God accomplish his decisive victory if transformation and reform now exist only on an individual level and not as worldwide accomplishments?

e. One reason it is difficult for us to deal with Moon's supposed claims to be a messiah is that we look at this issue from a post-Christian perspective rather than a pre-Christian one. That is, the early church changed the role of messiah as they assigned it to Jesus, thus cutting themselves off from their Jewish roots. Moon represents a return to the pre-Christian notions of messiah, before it was "spiritualized" by the early church to explain Jesus' failure to fulfill the role of messiah as the people at the time expected. The Christians later made Jesus into an incarnation of God, "fully God." This is not what *messiah* means in the Old Testament, and Moon feels that the early church changed this to account for their own failure to support Jesus and to explain why the expected kingdom had not been inaugurated. Messiahship is not a claim to be Jesus-as-the-Christ (to use Tillich's term). It is a return to the Jewish expectation of a human leader elected by God who will guide his chosen people in the restoration of the lost kingdom.

Of course, the Unification Church is subject to the same tendency to reinterpret pronouncements if plans do not go as expected. I am sure they would respond well to success and public acceptance and prestige, since they seek it. When attack and persecution come, you will note that their response is to say, "This is what we expected." Religiously, we all seem to demand too much in the early days. This attracts followers, but, when the plan runs into trouble, we "spiritualize" the failure of the overt success we expected but which was not forthcoming. Messiahs demand a lot from us. Our task is to explain our failure to live up to their expectation.

11. *The Unification Church is a bogus religious institution using spiritual doctrine to mask political and economic ambitions.*

a. In my travels, study, and interviews, I came to only two firm conclusions: (1) The movement is genuinely spiritual in its origins, at least as much so as any other new religious movement; and (2) it probably will establish itself as a long-term movement of some solidarity. I could, perhaps, have been "sold a bill of goods," but all the testimony in Korea points to its authentic origin in an intensely spiritual and religiously prolific time. Reverend Moon's authenticity as a religious leader is clouded by his later success and the general lack of acceptance of his program. The movement may develop new paths or go astray, but there seems no reason to question its origin in a time of religious ferment. Certainly Koreans see it this way. Even those who oppose it violently accept it as a competing religion.

b. A cloud comes over this question because of the unabashed political aims of the movement. Whether one accepts the goals or not, we should understand why a religious movement thinks it must enter the political and economic realm with its own programs in order to bring God's kingdom on earth. It is not the first religion with a political platform, and it is not likely to be the last. When we recall our own history, we observe that the United States was founded in an argument over theocracy.

Has the movement committed grievous political and financial sins that mark it as unacceptable and not a creditable religion? There are many complex questions concerning acts of impropriety to which I do not know the answer, but I have no reason to convict anyone in advance of the evidence. I understand why the movement finds political and economic involvement crucial to its task, and I think this path is full of risks and pitfalls. They know that too, but it is their way. I am sure errors have been made. The issue is whether those were intentional and whether they involve any "Moongate cover-up" operations. I tend to

195

doubt it, but gaining a definitive answer involves detective talents far more sophisticated than mine.

c. One religion writer for a leading newspaper said, "I think the Moonies deserve all the bad press they get." And so they do—on the whole. Their tactics are often questionable and often cause some people to get hurt in the rush. But, there is also a quieter, more spiritual side to the movement, which the press usually misses. Complication arises because the Moonies cast their activities in a highly spiritual light, whereas they do not appear in that light to the public. For instance, Moon gives a religious explanation for his Nixon defense, but at the same time, he hoped that by leading Nixon to call the nation to repentance, the Unification Church would gain prominence and power.

Are infiltration tactics unacceptable, or are they a necessary religious practice? Jesus is seen as having lacked a "battle plan"; the Moonies have one. The conspiratorial air about the Moon movement which bothers many stems largely from the battle-strategy mentality the Principle encourages. Satan's spiritual forces are real and subtle. If we are to win for God we must be as astute in our maneuvers as Satan is in his. This marshalling of human, Godly forces requires an uncanny use of power and skill. We recognize this as either necessary or legitimate in business and in politics, but is it offensive when it appears in religion? Or, is the one who will not take up a battle stance simply condemning himself to be ineffective and thus conceding the victory to Satan by default?

12. *The movement is totalitarian, authoritarian, and even fascist, resembling in its structure the Hitler Youth movement, and is a threat to democracy.*

a. One strange fact to note at the outset is that the movement's literature frequently mentions democracy in laudatory terms. It opposes Marxist dictatorship and claims to oppose Communism because it would destroy democracy. Of course, Marxists claim democracy for themselves too, so we know that everything depends on how the term is used. As members indicate, the movement is authoritarian in the sense that they have sought for and now accept a source of authority and willingly bind themselves to it. However, their loyalty is as much to the Principle as to the man, a fact hard for any outsider to determine.

b. The charge of similarity to the Hitler Youth is more difficult to deal with, because it involves both understanding the origins of the Hitler Youth movement and predicting changes in the direction the Moon movement might yet undergo. Hitler Youth, we forget, began as an idealized and almost spiritual search for new ethics in the midst of degeneration. It turned militant only later. The Unification Church is international, not nationalistic, for one thing, and it is antimilitaristic. The lurking question is whether it might change if its ambitions or timetable were thwarted. Would it then become less peaceful too? One member states, "I think the church will disband before it becomes militant."

c. In assessing the right of the Unification Church to claim to support democracy as we know it in America, one must remember the theme of Reverend Moon's bicentennial campaign and city tours. America is faltering morally and spiritually, and he has come to call us back to our task, to seek regeneration before it is too late. Democracy in America is given to us as God's gift, a holy experiment, a trust we hold in store for all mankind. Given the grossly self-seeking view most citizens have of what democracy means today, there is something in this religious view to make us stop and think.

13. *Reverend Moon supports the Park regime in Korea and is in league with the Korean CIA in illicit schemes.*

a. This charge opens a large can of worms. As one senses the emotional reactions involved, one is led to reflect on the dubious human quality of liking to believe dirt about one's opponents. Our human frailty accepts the charges it wants to believe even when evidence is lacking. We do experience an ancient human, perhaps unconscious, desire to believe the worst about those of whom we don't approve.

b. First, we must ask what is the evidence of the church's KCIA connection? Church officials (Colonel Bo Hi Pak in particular) have denied the charges and demanded that evidence be produced. The maker of an accusation traditionally has the advantage of being believed first, over the defender. That is a built-in inequity in the world, which a democratic legal system is supposed to counterbalance. Does this mean that we may not expect such charges ever to be substantiated? I cannot answer that personally, but I do think it would take numerous Justice Department agents numerous hours to get anything like solid evidence. But let the investigation be carried out. We know that the church is not averse to entering the political arena. If it does, though its motives be pure as snow, it is likely to be stained with guilt by association, as every politician knows. The church's program invites antagonism and reprisal, but it does not shun dubious associations. Rather the church hopes to league them to God's cause.

c. A short exploratory trip to Korea does not qualify me as an expert on politics in the Orient, but it did teach me that the situation is more complex than most Americans have time to realize. Things look a little different standing on a tiny peninsula, one which has been overrun and conquered during much of its history, than they do looking out from Middle America. There is repression of civil liberties in Korea, and there is undoubtedly religious as well as general surveillance. As for dubious activities beyond this, I do not feel competent to answer. It is clear that Moon supports President Park as the preferable alternative to Communism. Civil libertarians not only disagree with Moon but condemn his associations and are suspicious of his motives if he does not speak out against Park.

d. As was explained to me, one does not do business in Korea without government sanction, and the church carries on its industrial affairs under government approval. It appears to be a marriage of convenience, which is enough to convict the church on the spot for those whose views on religion and politics differ. I found that all religions are somewhat suspect in Korea as potential sources of political disruption. The Unification Church was not only out of favor in its early years but was subjected to some persecution. Then, as it succeeded financially, government cooperation increased. Now, with the church's rising negative press in the United States, the Park government has pushed it to arm's length again and put their relationship on hold. Church members have trouble getting visas to leave the country now, they say, and they now talk darkly of expected repression. As this book went to the publisher, these fears were confirmed by the arrest of some of the church's leaders in Korea on charges of income-tax evasion. It is hard to see the church as joining the Park government in secret schemes at the same time its leaders are being arrested.

14. *Sun Myung Moon himself came from a shady past involving sex scandal, multiple legal and illegal marriages, and several arrests on various charges.*

The first thing to note here is a historical oddity: Every strong religious leader has been charged with sexual irregularities. Such stories surround Jesus too and survive in the early literature. We need a super-Freud to tell us why it is that religious leaders immediately draw stories of sexual impropriety. Even if proved, it is not quite certain what "early sins" tell us about present legitimacy, but there seems to be a feeling that this would invalidate the doctrine or disestablish the credibility of the teaching. When I asked followers what it would mean to them if the stories of early scandal should prove true, it is interesting to note that some replied it would make no difference. They maintain their loyalty on different grounds.

Many charges are published by religious competitors in Korea, but little evidence seems forthcoming. We confront the unseemly business of one religion discrediting another. I confess I draw back from this as the sin of self-righteousness and the lack of charity that has plagued Christianity and all religions throughout history. There is no question that Moon was arrested several times in the early days, in the North first and later in Seoul. These arrests are not only admitted but celebrated as persecution, which the leader must go through and overcome to pay the indemnity necessary to found the movement. It would seem best to evaluate the movement as it stands today if we lack concrete evidence of a legal quality concerning its past.

15. *The morality of the whole movement is questionable because of its tactics and deceptive practices.*

Fund raising and so-called front organizations are a main concern, as has been mentioned already. But it is the question of moral principle that we need to face directly. There have been cases of deception or lack of honesty in fund raising, and the issue is whether the ends justify the means. Of course, there is the official denial that deception is either condoned or advocated, but the deeper issue buried here involves the meeting of East and West.

Is the principle of loyalty to the leader the chief ethical goal above all others, and is it that by which the follower ultimately will be judged? In the West we do not tend to think this way and are more individualistic in our ethics. But Unification doctrine puts the blame for the failure to complete Jesus' mission to bring the kingdom of God to earth on the disloyalty of Jesus' disciples and those around him. Thus, dedication to the leader and the cause become the chief ethical norms by which the individual expects to be judged. We must recognize a possible conflict in Eastern and Western ethical priorities. God, according to this theology, will not save us individually but only through a leader whose salvation plan depends for its effectiveness on the pledged loyalty of those who join him. Here is the core of Unification Church's Eastern ethics and also the source of conflict for those with different priorities and a predilection for Western directness.

Where Did I Come Out?

Where do I, your author, stand? To report my personal opinion is not the point of this book. Nevertheless, the reader may wonder where I came out, and it may sharpen your own response if I indicate, very briefly, what my own conclusions are. In any strict, orthodox sense, Unification doctrine is a heresy, but we have all been around long enough to know that what is rejected today as heresy *may* become tomorrow's orthodoxy. Furthermore, unorthodox doctrines in any day have always served to shock us into awareness and to force us to be clear about our own beliefs. Otherwise, we probably would continue to drift. In my own mind, Sun Myung Moon has done this for me, and he should do it for you, too.

1. Particularly in Japan and Korea, I was always asked one question by my audience after I finished asking my questions of them: "Now that you know so much about our church, will you join?" I answered by saying, "Let me teach you something about your own doctrine. Sun Myung Moon came not to found another church among the churches but to call all Christians and all religions to unite. In that goal to overcome divisions and religious strife, I am one with you, and it doesn't matter which church I join." Observing the intense factionalism present in Korea, both culturally and religiously, it is easy to see how a native might feel overwhelmed with the need to put a stop to this and unite all mankind as brothers and sisters. However, for the moment, the irony is that this goal has bred hostility and spawned the traditional reaction heaped on any new competitor in the religious marketplace.

2. I see the movement inevitably evolving into another established church, and I am not sure this can be prevented, although constant reform and renewal can keep the original spirit alive. A theory to unite all religions always has had the effect of simply producing one more theory among the others, because we have to accept the theory before we can use it as a base on which to unite. And many will never set aside their existing doctrines and beliefs to make that first step. Perhaps there is no such thing as one doctrine that can unite all peoples. The very structures that make up our world may have to be torn down before that becomes possible. My own thought is that pluralism in religion will remain until God himself blows the whistle on us.

There are tendencies already at work in the movement to modify or play down questionable or controversial aspects of the doctrine. Almost every past philosophy and religion has faced the same split between the strict adherents and those who would modify the doctrine to suit more easily realizable standards. One central, early church figure told me that he advocates as a next step the move to popularize (my term) the doctrine so that it can reach the mass of people and not just those willing to give up everything for it.

As a curia—a professional management class—develops, the church will lose not only some of its crusade appeal but also its mobility and adaptability. As the youth come in off the streets and acceptable industries replace their primitive but successful efforts at fund raising, seminaries will be built and Ph.D.'s sought, and more standard forms of vocation and employment pursued. This takes the heat off the church as they slow recruitment to a less frantic pace, but it also gives the new church the problem of fighting its own internal vested interests. As the church becomes public-relations conscious, they will be forced to present a better image. One pays the price for these compromises by rewarding those within the church who have corporation-executive virtues vs. the pioneering spiritual saint and worker.

Are we watching the development of "the bishops game"? That is, is power being transferred from the primitive origins and early disciples to the emerging church professionals? Some early disciples are prominent still; others once important are now increasingly on the sidelines. The story is told that officials in Rome, puzzled by the rise of Christianity, sent for Jesus' family to be brought to Rome so that they could see the people involved in the origins of this new religion. In appearance they found them humble people, just as reported. However, that discovery made no difference. By this time, power in the emerging Christian church had come to reside in the established bishops and in their city centers, not in primitive Jerusalem. Will the late-coming professional church managers now take over from the primitive originals? This is a change every religion has faced once its day of spontaneous origin has passed.

The spiritual life and growth of Unification Church members is what the general public sees least. But as the church grows and standardizes, will its spiritual life decrease and day-to-day concerns tend to take over the stage, as happens in most religious institutions? Reverend Moon sets a spiritual tone internally in the church. When the time comes that he is no longer there, will anyone else be able to fulfill that function to keep alive the dynamics of their prayer and spiritual life? The church in Korea is less vigorous in proportion to its distance from its origins, but the movement is still new in most other countries, except Japan where it is settling into success too. Spiritual zeal has a natural tendency to wane as time dims its original spark.

3. "Indemnity" and "reparation" are Principle doctrines that indicate the necessity for humanity to make atonement before it will be possible to restore a decaying order. In severe and demanding religious groups, this can lead to excessive self-punishment in an attempt to set the conditions. If we do not stress the necessity for human sacrifice, on the other hand, this leads to a too easy religious life. However, I cannot accept the notion that any indemnity paid by any human being, even a major providential figure, is sufficient to set the conditions that will free me or any portion of human society. The Moonies side with liberal theology in rejecting the notion of Jesus-as-God, but behind that traditional trinitarian idea is the conviction that only God has sufficient power to forgive and restore. Man can do much, but I am convinced only God can break the bonds that hold human society on its present, partially destructive course.

Is the source of human sin single or multiple? Whether or not we accept the account of the origin of sin given in the Principle, many members testify to the power that stems from discovering the primary source and cause of sin. If we know sin's single origin, we can be effective in combating it and perhaps overcome evil to restore mankind. However, Freud thought the origin of mental illness to be singular, and thus one method (his) could be effective to accomplish a cure. Today, we have become more pluralistic in our views about the causes of illness, but our power to effect a cure in every case declines too. Thus, if the Principle is too

203

narrow in its account of the origin of sin, as I believe it is, and if the sources of sin are actually many rather than one, the Moon program to eliminate sin falls under question. Plural sources are harder to control, and they perhaps defy human power. We cannot work effectively on so many fronts at once.

Will human beings accomplish what God cannot do alone? I think Reverend Moon rightly challenges us to sacrifice, to pursue spiritual training, and to redouble our effort—more than many nondemanding theologies require. My main disagreement comes over the interpretation of the human share in the power to influence events. The Unification Church divides the power by the formula 95 percent God's effort and 5 percent man's, stressing that the human 5 percent is absolutely crucial to the success or failure of the plan for restoring the kingdom of God on earth. Individually, I think, people can lock God out and block his operations. The key is to become open to God's work. In the end, the forces of destruction and deterioration on the loose in the world are more than people can tame or bend to God's use, I believe. A divinely empowered reordering of more cosmic proportions is required before all corruption shall cease. And I think this can only happen when God steps in and—in ways and by instruments I do not think I can predict—seizes control. I believe he has the power to do this and will enter in again at the moment he chooses. The question is, Is now the time of his choice?

4. Did Reverend Moon receive a revelation, and is he a genuine prophet? I have no trouble in accepting the genuineness of Reverend Moon's early experience. I think revelations are multiple, and God is able to work through many media. The question is whether I accept the content of the revelation, and here I can accept some aspects and not others. Sun Myung Moon seems to me to be a prophet come to call the world to repent as others have before. Clearly, he is spiritually gifted and is able to exercise a profound and often beneficial effect on his followers. He invites greater-than-life projections of both human ideals and human evils to be thrust upon his image. I see no reason to doubt his

sincerity. In fact, it is rather hard to account for his effectiveness if he does not believe in himself. As most who meet him testify, he is not an impressive individual on first meeting. It is what he projects that people respond to.

In the words of a familiar hymn, "The Lord hath yet more light and truth to break forth from His Word." With the Unification Church we face the question of whether revelation is closed or can continue. But the church's members also face the question themselves. One early witness to the formation of the *Divine Principle* has suggested that the book must now be revised. Will the church and Reverend Moon cease to be receptive to God's new message in a new day, as it accuses other established churches of having done? If it does, it will freeze itself around the perceptions given to it at an earlier day and time. Once established, it takes great strength to stay open to possible new light and change. There is a natural tendency to split into the reformists on the one side and the professional priests on the other. These tensions are not missing in the Moon movement.

5. Do we live in a decisive time, when changes that were not possible before are now open to us? Although I do not find their numerology or historical analysis very compelling, exploring the Moon movement is instructive because many members comment on and feel convinced of the apocalyptic quality of our time. From a Christian perspective, one certainly cannot deny that "the time is now." How and when God will move to bring history to a climax I do not know, but I do believe that we are told to be ready and always to be receptive to such a movement. The Unification timetable is too specific and ahead of itself for my money, but I do believe there are times when significant change is open to us.

Is, then, Reverend Moon the messiah come once again, "the Lord of the Second Advent"? I will conclude by saying a little more about what I think God's relationship to Sun Myung Moon may be. If God once chose the Jews—an unlikely choice considering their powerlessness—it is not beyond my ken that he could choose Moon. God can bend any instrument he chooses to his use, I believe. I have commented above on the subleties involved in making any direct claim about Moon. Following that formula, I am quite content to wait out time to see if Moon does enlarge his role as some predict. In the meantime, I am driven to reflect on what form God's action might take and how I might be able to detect his movement when it comes. If Moon is "of God" he cannot be stopped. If he is not, the movement will fade away. Time and God will tell.

6. In spite of the harm some members have suffered from whatever causes, I believe it possible for the movement—at least at times—to create a genuinely loving atmosphere and an international family bound by a desire to serve others and not themselves. Living in the midst of what surely must be one of the most self-centered and pleasure-seeking societies on the face of the globe, to experience that spirit is refreshing. I welcome it wherever it exists, whether in Moon centers or in my local Congregational church. I do not like to stress doctrine as a test (whether Moon's or Calvin's), and I accept Jesus' words that we will know his disciples because we see that they love one another. We have all watched in horror as our churches swell with self-righteousness and even hate. I find Jesus' followers wherever I experience selfless love extended in his name. Some are in Moon centers; many are not.

I think there will be a shift away from Moon's controversial doctrinal side and an increased stress on the practical "family life." Again, like Mormonism, which exalts its way of life as much as the defensibility of its doctrine on purely intellectual terms, life-style will increasingly become the focus of belief and the chief attraction for Moonies. An original primitive and powerful view seems immediately to be carried to extremes and to generate quarrels. The problem becomes modifying these excesses which were allowed to breed in the developing period. The excitement of the early challenge is lost, however, when the novel pattern of life becomes the focus of attention.

7. Have the established churches failed, so that God now must raise up some other instrument if his mission to

humanity is to be carried on? If we look around us, it is clear that Christian organizations have not yet established the kingdom of heaven on earth fully. History reports the church's constant apostasy in its mission to convey self-less love, service, and charity to all people. In American religious history, new evangelical surges often erupt outside established circles, and the rise of such groups as the Mormons and the Christian Scientists against bitterness and hostility are part of our national religious story, as Quakerism is in England. I think many churches are failing in their mission and have lost both a sense of the gospel and their appeal to the young. Reverend Moon arrives as a judgment on our religious failure and complacency—and that is painful for us to accept.

8. Is there such a thing as "spiritual openness"? Traveling in Moon circles one sees that many members now feel open to spiritual communication in ways in which they did not before. This change stems from the Korean tradition of belief in an active spirit world, but in any case the reported phenomena are numerous and frequent. The Moonie dreamworld is a busy place. Again, without appraising either the accuracy of these reports or their credibility, the strength of Moon spirituality does raise the question of whether we pedestrian Westerners have closed ourselves off from spiritual receptivity and whether there is a way we could become open once again. The early scientific age wanted desperately to deny spiritual perception as a threat to its empirical assumptions, but recently science seems to have loosened its stranglehold on us. If so, we should ask, How might we recover spiritual openness?

9. Do we like what we have become? New religious orders usually spring up when a society becomes dissatisfied with itself. Do you remember the *New Yorker* cartoon showing two middle-aged, well-to-do New Yorkers standing outside their Fifth Avenue apartment waiting for a taxi, dressed in mod clothes, beads, and the whole bit? One of them says to the other, "I don't think I like what we have become." Well, Reverend Moon is implicitly asking us, Do you really like what you have become? A *Playboy* ad tells us

that the young generation of the seventies is different from the drop-out-of-society youth of the sixties. The theme of this ad is that today we are sophisticated in debauchery and skilled in living for the moment's enjoyment alone with never a thought for the future. Is that really what we have become? And if it is, do we like it? A self-centered, idealless generation concentrating on self-satisfaction is surely barely one step short of civilization's collapse. Moonies challenge us to find an alternative idealism.

10. I think the doctrine will be (forcibly) "de-mythologized" as the predicted events and dates come and go, assuming, of course, that no obvious confirming change occurs. One can already detect backpaddling by some members to protect themselves against an outcome already less overt than the change they anticipated. The doctrine is historically explicit, and certain dates and victories (1981, for example) are predicted. Thus, we have the unusual opportunity to watch a religion grow and also reach its climactic events in our lifetime. If these forecasts are not literally fulfilled, something must be done to save the doctrine and preserve the church's life. Obviously this will be less exciting than the full realization of the physical kingdom of God now.

Experiencing the birth of a new religion firsthand makes one view the New Testament in a new light. Scholars rightly spend their time tracing back extant passages to earlier origins and comparing various versions of the gospel as we have received them. But suddenly one wonders: What kind of mass of material and sayings did our present slender volume emerge from? Antagonists pick out Moon sayings they either deride or abhor. But we have seen that it is also possible to select a much more spiritual, loving literature out of the mass of his sayings. In the New Testament, are we dealing with Jesus' "better sayings," when, in fact, if we had followed him during his public ministry, would we also have heard extravagant and questionable sayings? Must messiahs overstate their case and leave it to later generations to filter out the acceptable gospel? If Jesus stood center stage in Madison Square

Garden reciting an unedited version of the Gospel of John, would it fall on our ears differently than it does when we hear a distilled version in a now holy volume quietly read?

11. Why are the young attracted to Sun Myung Moon, and what core of genuineness do they find in his teaching? In an era of self-seeking, I think they are attracted by the demand for selfless devotion to a cause to usher in the new world of God's kingdom now for all people. What they learn to give is love, although many fail that lesson. As in most religions, the young are undoubtedly attracted for various reasons, including the wrong reasons. When they discover this and realize the demand being placed on them for self-sacrifice, they get out, but then they must explain away their earlier emotional enthusiasm. It is hard to learn to give love rather than always seeking it. It is difficult constantly to think of others ahead of oneself, and the normal human desire to rest a little creeps in. Still, every individual who joins Sun Myung Moon is a judgment both on our self-seeking society and on our established religious organizations for failing to provide a more attractive alternative channel for this youthful energy.

One reflection stands out after my study of the Moon movement: At least some of our young people today are looking for discipline, structure, strong parental figures, and they are willing to pour their commitment into a life of sacrifice and missionary zeal. Which of our current institutional churches, save perhaps the evangelical groups, has much missionary thrust these days? I know people who make a point of saying that we should not go out and try to convert others. Yet religious movements are strongest and most attractive when they have something they want so much to share with others that they accost people on the streets Moonie-style.

Our current majority life-style has succeeded in turning off at least some young people. They no longer want to continue that kind of self-centered existence. Liberally oriented outside observers see the structure of the Moonies' life as a threat, because they do not like its authoritarian aspects. But this appraisal assumes that acceptance of authority is somehow always bad. We have torn down most of the structures in our society and in our schooling that stressed discipline. This puts an immense burden on the individual, since he or she must now develop his or her own discipline internally. Some are strong enough and can do that, but many are not. The intense work schedule Moonie life requires points to the search for discipline many of the young are engaged in today.

When I first began studying the Moon movement, I had just returned from a sabbatical in Japan. I had gone there to study Zen Buddhism in Kyoto and to lead a discussion group on Western mysticism for a seminar of Japanese professors. Out of this came a little book, *Love Beyond Pain* (Paulist Press, 1977). After comparing and discussing Zen and certain strains of Western mysticism, I was convinced that both shared a common aim, though approached by different means. Mysticism, both Eastern and Western, expresses the need for the reform of the natural self. As it stands in society, human nature defeats itself. Its own ego looms too large on the horizon, thus obscuring its proper view of nature and other selves.

The conversion of love, I stated in my book, is what we need, so that love can become outgoing and not self-centered. Zen proposes one way to accomplish this, Christianity another, but both agree on the need for basic reformation of the self before any good can come out of it. As I began to study Sun Myung Moon, I was amazed to find this same core of teaching. At the end of my study, it is still my conviction that this aim of selfless, outgoing love is the basic Christian theme. And it is what young people of all races have discovered in Sun Myung Moon to the benefit of at least some of them.

12. Must the doctrine be wholly true for people to be benefited? After reading the stories of the personal havoc that followed in the wake of the spread of the Unification Church, what caused me to puzzle was hearing Moonies report in my interviews their debt to the Principle for changing their lives. This does not prove the doctrine's truth, but it forces us to balance the testimony of benefit

against the reports of personal destruction. Must we deny the possibility of personal change for the better if we cannot accept the doctrine? Is the correspondence between doctrine and personal help that neat and tight?

Freud was dogmatic in defending the truth of his analytical theory. However, if we do not accept it as gospel, there is no need to deny that its use often produces a cure. When you ask Moonies, "What attracted you to the movement?" a majority reply immediately, "the warmth and genuineness of the people." In psychiatry, the therapist may be responsible for the patient's cure more as a person than as a psychiatrist, and surely no psychiatrist would say his rate of cure is 100 percent or should be. The "ideal family" created by Moon doctrine in the centers where it is successful may provide the cure of souls the new convert seeks. If so, the convert naturally testifies to his indebtedness to the source, however we may appraise the merit of the doctrine.

During one weekend session I attended, the leader asked how his small group liked "the family," and one guest replied calmly, "I see that you have a community genuinely open and that you love each other. That's great, but I still have questions about the ideas and the doctrines." I do not mean to suggest that we should somehow divorce practical religion from theology, but I do think it is an interesting fact to observe that genuine personal benefits may be involved for some even if we are not ready to buy the doctrine lock, stock, and barrel. Of course, Moonies feel they have found the truth, but the proof for this tends to come in the form of their testimony of personal change. To say this is not to prejudge either where the power comes from or the movement's eventual success or failure. But the projected ideal of bringing the kingdom of God on earth is the instrument by which emotions can be converted from self-destruction and personal energy harnessed to many goals. The cloud hanging over the movement is that the outcome for some people has been negative.

Postscript: Is God Using Reverend Sun Myung Moon?

Bye and Bye, when the morning comes,
All the saints of God are gathered home.
We'll tell the story of how we've overcome,
And we'll understand it better bye and bye.

—from a hymn sung in the Unification Church

The Principle teaches that we should believe there are many providential events. Those of us outside the movement seldom see the significance of the Madison Square Garden, Yankee Stadium, or Washington Monument rallies, for instance. These are not public relations extravaganzas. They are events that, Moonies feel, God's timetable dictates must take place to fulfill the necessary conditions for human salvation and God's release from suffering. In every center all over the world I found posters about the rallies and intense interest in these "providential" events which few from overseas would ever attend. I was once introduced to speak to members as someone "providential" to the church. I am not at all sure about that designation, but I am sure that showing *Man of La Mancha* as the movie at the Belvedere estate on Children's Day in November of 1976 was a providential event for me.

We had been up since early morning listening to Reverend Moon speak and celebrating Children's Day with several thousand on the lawn for lunch. In the afternoon the fun and games began, "a religious Woodstock," my guide informed me. Since I was cold and had already played one game of Moonie dodge ball at the Boonville training center, my guide suggested sitting down to watch the movie being shown in the garage. *Man of La Mancha* presents a

212

somewhat tortured version of the story of Don Quixote. As the sad struggle of this man who has dreams out of keeping with his crude and prosaic surroundings unfolds, it builds toward the famous song "The Impossible Dream." I am not a crying man by nature, but I nearly wept over the poignancy of the setting.

> To dream the impossible dream,
> To fight the unbeatable foe,
> To bear with unbearable sorrow,
> To run where the brave dare not go. . . .
> To right the unrightable wrong,
> To love pure and chaste from afar,
> To try when your arms are too weary,
> To reach the unreachable star!

I do believe that Reverend Moon has a better chance to realize his dream than the man of La Mancha, but ultimately it is—to me—an impossible dream to bring the kingdom of God on earth—now, by our effort, to bend the powers of economics and culture and intellect to God's service. Yet the song is popular today because it speaks to the idealism of our generation in trying nonetheless to realize the impossible dream. I do think much may be accomplished even if the full dream itself eludes our realization. Of course, humans often become desperate when they try to reach something beyond their power, and to this flaw I would attribute most of the movement's past errors.

The song's significance goes deeper than futile idealism if we cast the "impossible dreamer" into the context of God's providential operations. First we have to ask: Is God using Sun Myung Moon to bring us a message or to accomplish a purpose, even if it is not the literal message the Unification Church reads, or not even the one Sun Myung Moon himself understands? There are, in this movement, more lessons for those interested in religious phenomena than have been offered to us in some days. God may be challenging us through Moon, even if most of us fail to read the challenge correctly and prefer to defend our original basic assumptions without further examination. Perhaps

God never moves directly but only indirectly. If we "correct" Reverend Moon, we may learn more about God's message for the day than God could or wants to reveal to us directly.

There is latent religious significance for us, if we can discover the truth contained in a heresy when it is a powerful one. However, the most fundamental question is: Will God save Reverend Sun Myung Moon and his movement? In almost every interview question session, I began by asking, "What attracted you to the Unification Church?" Then I ended by asking, "What will you do if events do not turn out in your lifetime as you expect?" I went on to explain that I was not being hostile but merely propounding my theory that every significant religious movement or individual religious experience must go through many crucifixion days when its early and perhaps superficial hopes are thwarted. Only at that point does the test of faith begin, in the wake of the destruction of an early and too easily elicited enthusiasm.

One member said to me once, half in jest and half in earnest, that his test of faith in the church would be to follow the church's custom and allow his marriage to be arranged for him following Reverend Moon's version of the Oriental system. That is a minor test of faith for members compared to what will happen if days come and go and the world does not change its basic character. Of course, I do not know with certainty that this will happen to them. But if their dream does not come about, that will be the test of the movement, not marriage or fund raising or the threat of kidnapping and deprogramming. Will Reverend Moon, too, undergo his crucifixion experience, not literally, like Jesus, but spiritually?

Of course, we know Moonies do not claim the events they predict are predestined. These providential events can fail or be postponed due to human disloyalty. However, if at the end of the twentieth century, the world retains its basic outer structure, then, no matter how rich the spiritual side benefits, the actual coming of their Kingdom will have undergone crucifixion once again. As I explained in asking my question to the members, Christianity, in my view, was first born out of the disciples' crushed hopes and next out of the early church's unfulfilled expectations of Jesus' return in their own lifetime. They weathered that experience and learned to see God's hand moving in these events in a way to which they had been blind in the enthusiasm to see their ideal hopes realized immediately.

The Holy Spirit Association for the Unification of World Christianity is hardly thirty years old. If you consider its youth, it already has an amazing history. But its real birth, I think, is yet to come, as is the real test of Reverend Moon's faith in God and his followers' faith in God's providential plan. If God has often acted in unusual ways, in unexpected times and places, it is not too odd that a new Israel should arrive in a fractional Korean people or that Sun Myung Moon should feel himself called as God's spokesman. The question is whether he is conveying a message from God that still today is hidden beneath his overt doctrine. The crucial events that will tell us this have yet to be acted out.

"Amazing grace, how sweet the sound, that saved a wretch like me." The Unification Church claims that

Planned World Headquarters for the Unification Church to be built in Seoul on Yoido Island.

spiritual blessings and gifts have come to it, which I have no reason to deny. But, will God yet pour out his grace on this movement, even though they have not asked for it? Will he raise up their literal hopes after they are dashed so that they, in their turn, can become a new witness to God's action to rescue human failure? Its enemies testify to the failure of human power within the church, perhaps too darkly. But the question is: Will God step in to restore destruction when the Moonies' human power fails or runs amuck? We are once again witnessing the age-old religious drama unfold, and we may yet live through the climactic chapter in our own time.

Bibliography

Books

American Committee for Human Rights of Japanese Wives of North Korean Repatriates. *If I Had Wings Like a Bird: Letters from Japanese Wives*. New York, 1974.

Bach, Marcus. *Strangers at the Door*. Nashville: Abingdon, 1971.

Bjornstad, James. *Moon Is Not the Son: A Close Look at the Religion of Rev. Sun Myung Moon*. Minneapolis: Bethany Fellowship, 1977.

Choi, Sang I. K. *Principles of Education: Theory of Origins of Crimes*. 2 vols. San Francisco: Re-education Center, 1969, 1970.

Edward, George, ed. *The Way of the World*. Washington, D.C.: Holy Spirit Association for the Unification of World Christianity (HSA-UWC), 1974.

Enroth, Ronald. *Youth Brainwashing and the Extremist Cults*. Grand Rapids, MI, 1977.

Fackre, Gabriel. *Word in Deed: Theological Themes in Evangelism*. Eerdmans, 1975.

Freedom Leadership Foundation. *Communism: A New Critique and Counter-Proposal*. Washington, D.C., 1975.

Holy Spirit Association for the Unification of World Christianity. *Holy Songs*. Washington, D.C., n.d.

Hoffer, Eric. *The True Believer*. New York: Harper & Brothers, 1951.

Jones, W. Farley, ed. *Unification Church: As Others See Us*. HSA-UWC, 1974.

Kim, Young Ong. *Divine Principle and Its Application*. HSA-UWC, 1968.

———. *Unification Theology and Christian Thought*. New York: Golden Gate Publishing Co., 1975.

———. *World Religions*. 2 vols. New York: Golden Gate Publishing Co., 1976.

Korean Overseas Information Service. *Facts About Korea*. 1975.

Lee, Sang Hun. *The Way to Happiness: An Abstract of Unification Thought*. New York: Unification Thought Institute, 1975.

———. *Unification Thought*. New York: Unification Thought Institute, 1973.

Levitt, Zola. *The Spirit of Sun Myung Moon*. Irvine, CA: Harvest House Publishers, 1976.

Lipton, Robert. *Thought Reform and the Psychology of Totalism*. New York: Norton & Co., 1961.

Lofland, John. *Doomsday Cult.* Englewood Cliffs, N.J.: Prentice-Hall, 1966. An expanded and revised edition is forthcoming.

Meerloo, Joost. *The Rape of the Mind.* New York: World Publishing Co., 1956.

Michael, Franz H. *The Taiping Rebellion.* 3 vols. Seattle: University of Washington Press, 1966, 1971.

Moon, Sun Myung. *America in God's Providence.* New York: Unification Church of America, 1976.

————. *A Prophet Speaks Today.* New York: HSA-UWC, 1975.

————. *Christianity in Crisis: New Hope.* New York: HSA-UWC, 1974.

————. *Divine Principle.* New York: HSA-UWC, 1976.

————. *New Hope: Twelve Talks by Sun Myung Moon.* New York: HSA-UWC, 1973.

————. *The New Future of Christianity.* The Unification Church International, 1974.

————. *True Path to Peace: One God, One World, One Religion.* One World Crusade, 1972.

National Ad Hoc Committee, A Day of Affirmation and Protest. *A Day of Affirmation and Protest.* Pt. I: *A Meeting of Concerned Parents;* Pt. II: *The Unification Church: Its Activities and Practices.* National Ad Hoc Committee. . ., 1976.

Palmer, Spencer J. *Korea and Christianity.* Seoul, Korea: Hollym Corporation, 1967.

Patrick, Ted, with Dulack, Tom. *Let Our Children Go.* New York: Ballantine, 1977.

Professors World Peace Academy. *Strategy for Peace.* Japan, 1975.

Richardson, Herbert, ed. "Documents Concerning the Theology of the Unification Church." Dissertation, University of Toronto, 1976.

Sargant, William. *Battle for the Mind.* Garden City, N.Y.: Doubleday, 1957.

Shih, Vincent Y. C. *The Taiping Ideology.* Japan: University of Washington Press, 1967.

Streiker, Lowell D. *The Jesus Trip.* Nashville: Abingdon, 1971.

Unification Church. *Unification Church Farm: A Christian Cooperative.* Swindon, England, 1975.

————. *Songs for Worship and Fellowship.* Washington, D.C., n.d.

Unification Thought Institute. *Unification Thought: Study Guide.* 1975.

Unified Family Enterprises. *Statement of Purpose—Day of Hope: God Bless America Festival.* England: Unified Family Enterprises Ltd., 1976.

Weems, Benjamin B. *Reform, Rebellion and the Heavenly Way.* Tucson: University of Arizona Press, 1964.

Wells, David F., and Woodbridge, John, eds. *The Evangelicals.* Nashville: Abingdon, 1975.

Yamamoto, J. Isamu. *The Puppet Master.* Downers Grove, IL: Inter-Varsity Press, 1977.

Booklets and Pamphlets

Carter, Judith Harris. *A Personal Observation.* Norfolk, VA, 1975.

Durst, Mose. *The Creative Community Project.* Berkeley, CA, n.d.

Holy Spirit Association for the Unity of World Christianity. *One World Crusade* (pamphlet). Reading, England, n.d.

————. *One World Crusade* (booklet). Reading, England, n.d.

————. *Sun Myung Moon* (booklet outlining Moon's life history). New York, 1969.

————. *The Sun Myung Moon Foundation.* Reading, England, n.d.

————. *Return to the Christian Community.* Reading, England, 1973.

Moon, Sun Myung. *The Kingdom of the Future: An Introduction to the Divine Principle.* Reading, England: HSA-UWC, n.d.

Orme, Dennis F. *A Christian Manifesto for Our Land.* Reading, England: Federation for World Peace and Unification, 1975.

Unification Church of America. *Sun Myung Moon* (booklet describing Bicentennial activities). New York, 1976.

Unification Church Periodicals

Newsletter of the One World Crusade. Reading, England: One World Crusade, July 17, 1976.

New World Magazine. Barrytown, New York: Unification Theological Seminary, July 4, 1976.

Periodical and Newspaper Articles

Deprogramming

Burstein, Patricia. "Rabbi Maurice Davis." *People.* Dec. 13, 1976.

"Cult 'Deprogrammer' Receives Jail Sentence." *Washington Post.* July 7, 1976.

"Judge: Moon-Child is Not a Victim." New York *Daily News.* Sept. 24, 1975.

"Pam Goes Free." *The Hutchinson News* (Kansas). Dec. 5, 1975.

Tallyn, Cathy. "Deprogramming Moonies: Legal Hazard for Parents." *Contra Costa Times.*

"Tucson Center: Bringing the Cultists Back." *Los Angeles Times.* Jan. 1, 1977.

Willoughby, W. F. "'Deprogramming' Jesus Freaks and Others: Can America Tolerate Private Inquisitions?" *Christian Century.* May 2, 1973.

————. "A Futile Try to Deprogram a Believer." *Washington Star.* Sept. 3, 1975.

Ziegler, Mel. "The Man Who 'Deprograms' Moonies." *San Francisco Chronicle.* Dec. 12, 1975.

Ex-Moonies

Alcorn, Wallace. "Escape From Sun Myung Moon." *Moody Monthly.* May 1976.

Carroll, Jerry. "Disillusioned Disciples Tell Why They Quit." *San Francisco Chronicle.* Dec. 4, 1975.

Harayda, Janice. "I was a Robot for Sun Myung Moon." *Glamour.* April 1976.

Kemp, Gerard. "American Rescued From Sect Tells of Mindbending." *London Daily Telegraph.* May 4, 1976.

McGuire, Stryker. "A Nightmare Called Moon." *San Antonio Light.* Sept. 7, 1975.

Ross, Barbara. "Total Dedication Can be Blinding." *The Reporter Dispatch* (New York). June 9, 1975.

Tallyn, Cathy. "Ex-Moonies Tell How They Escaped." *Contra Costa Times.* Oct. 3, 1976.

Whitley, Stan. "Moon Follower Talks of Brainwashing Attempts." *Great Bend Tribune.* Oct. 14, 1975.

"Why I Quit the Moon Cult." In "Coping with Cults." *Seventeen Magazine.* June, 1976.

Parents

Blau, Eleanor. "Three Hundred Parents of Rev. Moon's Followers Meet in Washington to Seek Federal Investigation of Group." *New York Times.* Feb. 14, 1976.

Brozan, Nadine. "Moon Church: From Parents Who Approve." *New York Times.* Sept. 16, 1976.

Carroll, Jerry. "Parents Take on the Rev. Moon." *San Francisco Chronicle,* Dec. 8, 1975.

Davis, Maurice. "Moon People and Our Children." *Jewish Community Center Bulletin.* June 10, 1974.

Edwards, Charles H. "How I Rescued My Son From the Moonies." *Medical Economics.* Nov. 1, 1976.

Kemp, Gerard. "Parents Fight 'Brainwashing' by Bizarre Sect." *London Daily Telegraph.* May 3, 1976.

Tallyn, Cathy. "Parents vs. Unification Church: Their Kids Become Moonies." *Contra Costa Times.* Oct. 5, 1976.

Politics

Anderson, Jack. "Moon Troupe." *Philadelphia Bulletin.* Nov. 22, 1976.

Crittenden, Ann. "Moon's Sect Pushes Pro-Seoul Activities." *New York Times.* May 25, 1976.

Fraker, Susan, and Marro, Anthony. "Washington's Korea Lobby." *Newsweek.* Nov. 22, 1976.

Horowitz, Irving L. "Science, Sin, and Sponsorship." *Atlantic.* March 1977.

Horrock, Nicholas M. "Aide to Moon Denies Press Charges." *New York Times.* Nov. 2, 1976.

Kirk, Donald. "Dirty Tricks Korean Style." *Saturday Review.* Jan. 8, 1977.

Lewis, Anthony. "Sauce for the Gander." *New York Times.* Nov. 11, 1976.

Marks, John D. "From Korea With Love." *Washington Monthly.* February 1974.

Riley, John. "The Korean CIA's Reign of Terror In Southern California." *New West.* Nov. 22, 1976.

Schmelzer, Rolf. "Sektierer in der Politik" (Sect in Politics). *Vorwarts* (West Germany). July 15, 1976.

Rallies

Blau, Eleanor. "Moon Rally Draws 25,000, Half Stadium Capacity." *New York Times.* June 2, 1976.

Borger, Gloria. "Even a Messiah Needs a P.R. Man in Washington." *Washington Star.* Sept. 13, 1976.

———. "Threatened Competition Has 'Moonies' Worried." *Washington Star.* Sept. 15, 1976.

Culver, Virginia. "Rev. Moon Plans June Stadium Extravaganza." *Denver Post.* April 23, 1976.

"Fifty Thousand at Rally by Rev. Sun Myung Moon." *Los Angeles Herald Examiner*. Sept. 20, 1976.

Kemp, Gerard. "God Bless America Banquet Organized by Moon Sect." *London Daily Telegraph*. May 6, 1976.

Knight, Athelia. "Marchers Oppose U.S. Vietnam Stand." *Washington Post*. April 6, 1976.

Meyer, Eugene L. "Moon's Million Dollar Rally." *Washington Post*. Sept. 12, 1976.

Meyer, Eugene L., and Johnson, Janis. "Moon Festival Draws 50,000 to Monument"; "This May Be a Chance to See Our Daughter." *Washington Post*. Sept. 14, 1976.

Smith, J. Y. "Moon Followers Clean Up Area After Festival." *Washington Post*. Sept. 20, 1976.

"Sun Myung Moon Ends Ministry in the U.S. with Anti-Communist Speech in Capitol." *New York Times*. Sept. 20, 1976.

Cults, Religious Movements

"Cultism and the Young: Security blanket staves off time and adult responsibility." *Frontiers of Psychiatry*. Sept. 1, 1976.

Heim, S. Mark. "'Divine Principle' and the Second Advent." *Christian Century*, May 11, 1977.

"Irrational Behavior or Evangelical Zeal?" *Chronicle of Higher Education*. Oct. 18, 1976.

Japanese Religions. July 1976. Published by Center for the Study of Japanese Religions. Kyoto, Japan. Three articles discussing the Unification Church appear in this issue.

Johnson, Janis. "Spiritual Renewal May Be in First Stages in America, Study Finds." *Washington Post*. July 23, 1976.

Lyles, Jean Caffey. "Letting Go: Everybody Has the Right to Be Wrong." *Christian Century*. May 11, 1977.

"New Messiahs Attract Youth." In Campus Ministry Program Packet. Chicago, IL: Campus Ministry Communications. A summary of several religious groups, including a descriptive article on the Unification Church by Jane D. Mook from *A.D.* (May 1974).

Reel, William. "Religion and the Moonies." *New York Daily News*. May 25, 1976.

"Religious Cults: Newest Magnet for Youth." *U.S. News and World Report*. June 14, 1976.

Roiphe, Anne. "Why Do Kids Follow the Rev. Sun Myung Moon? Are We Too 'Open' Now?" *Vogue*. November 1976.

Unger, Arthur. "Tough-Talking 'Closeup on New Religions.'" *Christian Science Monitor*. Sept. 1, 1976.

"Why Kids Join Cults." *Woman's Day*. February 1977.

General

Aikawa, Takaaki. "The Current Scene." *Japanese Christian Quarterly*. Spring 1975.

Bernstein, Paula. "Rabbi Sheds Light on the Moon Struck. Moon Power is No Myth." *New York Daily News*. June 1, 1976.

Blasdale, Jean. "The Strange Cult of the Reverend Moon." *The Review of the News*. June 9, 1976.

Sun Myung Moon and the Unification Church

Blau, Eleanor. "Moon Followers Have Solidified Their Base Here and Now Look for Respectability." *New York Times*. Oct. 1, 1975.

Carmody, John. "A Look At 'Moonies': Money, Politics and Confusion." *Washington Post*. Sept. 2, 1976.

Chandler, Russell. "By the Light of the 'Saviourly' Moon." *Christianity Today*. March 1, 1974.

"Clergy Denounce Rev. Moon." *Detroit Free Press*. Dec. 29, 1976.

Cotter, John. "Bizarre Plot to Rule the World." *San Francisco Examiner*. Nov. 30, 1975.

———. Series in the *New York Daily News*. Nov. 30–Dec. 4, 1975: "Sun Myung Moon: Missionary or Menace?"; "Four Days as a Child of Sun Myung Moon"; "How Moon Wins Hearts and Minds"; "Moonism: There Isn't an Easy Way Out"; "Is the Tide About to Turn On Sun Myung Moon?"

Cowley, Susan C. "Moon Rising." *Newsweek*. May 26, 1975.

Dart, John. "Cult's Goal: 'Power to Rev. Moon.'" *Los Angeles Times*. Jan. 29, 1976.

"Darker Side of Sun Moon." *Time*. June 14, 1976.

Davis, Neil. "No Fund Raising Deception Found." *Burlington Free Press* (Vermont). Nov. 5, 1976.

Dougherty, Philip H. "The Rev. Sun Myung Moon, 'Good Client'" [advertising]. *New York Times*. Sept. 30, 1976.

Dugan, George. "Moon Movement Opens Seminary." *New York Times*. Sept. 21, 1975.

Eisner, Peter. "Neighbors Favor Moon Church." *Poughkeepsie Journal*. Sept. 11, 1975.

"Father Won't Meet with Daughter He Calls Kidnapped." *Oakland Tribune*. Oct. 3, 1976.

Geppert, Hans J. "Der Gott, der die Gehirne Mäscht" (The God that Brainwashes). *Deutsches Allgemeines Sonntags Blatt*. May 9, 1976.

Gray, Janis. "Mr. Moon and His Church." *Claremont Courier*. Dec. 25, 1976.

Halloran, Richard. "Tourism in Korea: Korea?!" *New York Times*. Dec. 3, 1976.

Hoffman, David. Series in the *Evening Journal*, Wilmington, DE. Nov. 29–Dec. 2, 1975: "Unification Church Doctrines Center on Moon As Messiah"; "Cult is Active in Newark"; "Parents Unite Against Unification Church"; "Moon: From Murky Background to Founder of Cult"; "Moonie Cult Built on Army of Youth"; "Moon's Eden on Hudson Inspires Rumors, Tax Wars, Few Intimacies."

"In Defense of Rev. Moon." Letters to the Editor, *Wall Street Journal*. June 21, 1976.

Jaeger, Harry J., Jr. "By the Light of a Masterly Moon." *Christianity Today*. Dec. 12, 1975.

Jones, Clayton. "Rev. Moon to Organize Movement in Europe." *Christian Science Monitor*. Sept. 17, 1976.

Kaiser, Charles. "Moon Sect Steadily Adds Properties to Its Domain." *New York Times*. Sept. 19, 1976.

Kang, Wi Jo. "The Influence of the Unification Church in the U.S.A." *Missiology*. January 1975.

Klaidman, Stephen. "Moon Is Cheered by Scientists at Symposium He Sponsored." *Washington Post*. November 1976.

Knoble, John. "Moonie, Deprogrammer Trade Swipes." *New Haven Register.* Nov. 21, 1976.

Kwitny, Jonathan. "A U.S. Agency's Act May Eclipse Crusade of Moon." *Wall Street Journal.*

Landes, Marie-Gisele. "Making of a Moonie." *Atlas World Press Review.* September 1976.

Longcope, Kay. "Disillusionment Eroding Rev. Moon's 'Family.'" *Boston Globe.* April 27, 1975.

Marty, Martin E. "Say It Ain't So Roger." *Christian Century.* June 25, 1975.

"Ministers Advice on 'Moonies.'" *Herald-Weekly* (Newton Falls, OH). July 21, 1976.

"Moon's Annual Science Meeting is Becoming a Tradition." *Science.* Dec. 17, 1976.

"Moon's Credibility Game." *Christian Century.* Sept. 24, 1975.

"Moon Seeks More Land for Empire." *Los Angeles Times.* June 26, 1976.

Peerman, Dean. "Korean Moonshine." *Christian Century.* Dec. 4, 1974.

Pond, Elizabeth. "Korean Freedoms Ebb." *Christian Science Monitor.* Sept. 2, 1974.

Post, Henry. "The Making of a Moon Man." *Harper's Weekly.* May 31, 1976.

Pousner, Michael. "Who's Afraid of Sun Myung Moon?" *Penthouse.* June 1976.

"Proclamation on the Activities Being Undertaken by the Unification Church." *Boston Globe.* Dec. 10, 1976.

Putney, Michael. "Rev. Moon: A Messiah—Or a Menace?" *National Observer.* June 12, 1976.

Rasmussen, Mark. "How Sun Myung Moon Lures America's Children." *McCall's.* September 1976.

"Re: June 14 article, 'Moon Children.'" (Letter to the Editor) *Newsweek.* July 4, 1976.

"Rev. Moon Aides Term Criticism Distorted, Unfair." *Los Angeles Times.* Dec. 30, 1976.

Rice, Berkeley. "Honor Thy Father Moon." *Psychology Today.* January 1976.

———. "The Pull of Sun Moon." *New York Times Magazine.* May 30, 1976.

Robbins, Thomas *et al.* "The Last Civil Religion: Reverend Moon and the Unification Church." *Sociological Analysis.* Summer 1975.

Ross, Scott. "The SON and Moon." *New Wine.* February 1975.

Rubenstein, Richard. Letter to the Editor, *New York Times.* Jan. 1, 1977.

Spears, Larry. "Attempt by Moonies to Buy San Francisco Hotel." *Oakland Tribune.* Jan. 9, 1977.

———. "Gifts Link Moon With Bay Figures." *Oakland Tribune.* Jan. 5, 1977.

Studer, Carolyn. "The Heresies of Rev. Moon." *Theolog.* Dec. 8, 1976.

"Sun Myung Moon—Troubles Build Up for the Mysterious Leader of the Unification Church." *People.* Jan. 3, 1977.

"Sun Myung Moon's Followers Say He Might Stay in U.S. for Three Years." *New York Times.* Sept. 22, 1976.

Tallyn, Cathy. "Recruitment Steps Up in Country: How Moonies Find Their Followers." *Contra Costa Times.* Oct. 6, 1976.

"Three Religious Groups Join In Attack on Moon's Church." *Los Angeles Times.* Dec. 29, 1976.

Walsh, John. "Meeting on Unity of the Sciences: Reflections on the Rev. Moon." *Science*. Sept. 19, 1975.

Welles, Chris. "Eclipse of Sun Myung Moon." *New York Magazine*. Sept. 27, 1976.

Whalen, William J. "Rev. Sun Myung Moon: Pied Piper of Tarrytown." *U.S. Catholic*. October 1976.

"What I Learned About Sun Myung Moon," Pts. 1–3 (interview with George W. Swope). *Christian Herald*. July–October 1976.

Whittemore, L. A. "Sun Myung Moon: Prophet for Profit." *Parade (Detroit Free Press)*. May 30, 1976.

Woodward, Kenneth L. *et al*. "Life With Father Moon." *Newsweek* (cover story). June 14, 1976.